# P.S. Kiss the Duchess for Me

# P.S. Kiss the Duchess for Me

*letters from an unknown soldier*

Edited and with commentary by
Joe Rossi

*P.S. Kiss the Duchess for Me: Letters from an Unknown Soldier*

Published by Hats Off Books®
610 East Delano Street, Suite 104
Tucson, Arizona 85705 U.S.A.
www.hatsoffbooks.com

*Publisher's Cataloging-In-Publication Data*
*(Prepared by The Donohue Group, Inc.)*

Moss, Joseph R.
    P.S. kiss the duchess for me : letters from an unknown soldier / [Joseph R. Moss] ; edited and with commentary by Joe Rossi.

    p. : ill. ; cm.
    ISBN: 1-58736-583-9

    1. Moss, Joseph R., 1911—Correspondence. 2. United States. Army—Biography. 3. Jewish soldiers—United States—Correspondence. 4. World War, 1939–1945—Personal narratives, American. 5. World War, 1939–1945—Personal narratives, Jewish. 6. World War, 1939–1945—Participation, Jewish. I. Rossi, Joe. II. Title: Kiss the duchess for me

D811 .M67 2006
940.548/1    2005937302

rev201401

For Jerry Anthony, Marilyn Alexia, and Christina Grace

# Contents

She doesn't know why she never read the letters. She remembers seeing them in the old, brown, metal strongbox. They had been there for some forty-seven years. She had glanced at some of the other contents of the box—the old envelopes containing outdated insurance papers, some old letters from his brothers.

When had her mother put them there, all 150, tied up in a white satin ribbon? Did she place one in each time she received it? Or did she do it after that day in September? Rosh Hashanah it was. Early evening, at twilight. She remembers the doorbell ringing, the Western Union deliveryman, the telegram. (Whatever happened to the telegram? Did her mother save it? She had saved the letters, the personal effects sent sometime later.)

"That must be from Joey," her mother said, "wishing us a happy New Year."

She remembers her mother's anguished cry, the slump to the ground. She remembers herself, at nine years old, for some reason running out the front door, falling to her knees onto the grass, hands clasped together in some sort of prayer.

*Marilyn "The Duchess" Rossi*

# Preface

Inside a box at my mother's house lay the sleeping ghost of the past, waiting to be awakened like a genie that hides inside a lamp, like a mystery that sits tucked away in a dusty attic. We're not sure how they ended up so neatly tied together and preserved, each letter sitting snugly inside its envelope. All we know is that we have them.

Joe Moss was my grandfather, my mother's father. He was the grandpa I would grow up knowing only through faded old photographs and anecdotes. The letters were his. And the letters tell a story.

This book was my mother's idea. Her working title had been *Letters from My Father*. In her possession were the 150 carefully preserved letters her mother, the late Gertrude Moss, had received from Private Joe Moss over a period of eight months as he worked his way through basic training, finally arriving in France during the summer of 1944, where the Allied invasion of Europe was underway. An unrepentant and unabashed romantic, he wrote to Gertie, as he called my grandmother, almost every day he was in the service.

He began his letters with "My Darling," and usually ended with a postscript asking Gertie to kiss their nine-year-old daughter for him. For years after his death, the letters remained in the brown metal strongbox, neatly tied together by the aforementioned white satin ribbon.

For my mother, reading the letters reintroduced her to a man she had known only as a father. "I came to know him as a husband, a cousin, an uncle, and as a friend," she said. They acquainted me with a man I had never known at all. I found myself transported back to the 1940s. It's like a time capsule, I thought. A good friend who read the letters corrected me: "It *is* a time capsule," she said.

We are there with him in the barracks undergoing basic training. We are there with him on the trains. We are there with him in the French countryside "with the roar of guns as a background." We are there with him at the USO watching the youngsters "jitterbug and go to it." We go to the movies with him, where he avoids any that deal with war. We rehearse with him as he and his fellow soldiers endeavor to stage a show for their camp. We learn how much he loved show business. One hope he always held out was that my mother, whom in his later letters he almost always referred to as "the Duchess," would make it in show business one day. As he hunkered down in those foxholes in France, he fretted about whether or not she was keeping up with her piano.

This book also provides us with an opportunity to experience World War II through the eyes of someone who would never see it as history. Others who served but survived, while also deserving our deepest respect, can only look back upon the war as something that happened in the past. Joe never had that luxury. His account is an immediate, first-person look at World War II and at a fate that was closing in on him.

One thing to keep in mind is that these are personal letters. Obviously, they were not written for a large audience. Therefore, there are references and situations he discusses that we will never really understand. We've done our best to try to fill in the blanks; but where we couldn't, you will have to use your own imagination.

Once I approached a publisher with hopes of publishing the complete collection of letters. He told me that because my grandfather wasn't famous, nobody wanted to hear his story. After all, he said, there are thousands of stories like his, and every soldier had a daughter they called their Duchess. That is my point. This is a story for the thousands of unsung heroes nobody will know about. Indeed, after my mother's death in 2001, I learned to what extent my mother had gone to bat for this manuscript, uncovering letters to Stephen Spielberg and Tom Brokaw among others.

What strikes me about the totality of this story is that it embodies everything that makes for good storytelling. A likeable but disadvantaged protagonist with dubious origins rises above his circumstances, musters up the courage to confront a difficult situation, and becomes a better man for it. It is the hero's journey through the long dark night of the soul. It is overflowing with romance, with humor, with undeniable charm, and with vivid imagery. It illuminates the bonds of blood that are unbreakable even in times of war.

Based on the fact that countless strangers, knowing little about my mother or me, have written to say how moving they found the manuscript, I have to believe there is a larger audience for this work. And when you read the letters and get to know Joe, you will no doubt see that, as I have mentioned, he loved show business. So yes, I think he would dig this; he really would. He is the star of this show.

Some further notes about these letters. Joe tended to write in fragments. My spelling and grammar checker just about went nuts with "fragment consider revising." Well, fragments are the way my grandfather wrote, and I wish to remain true to his conversational tone. I have edited out quite a few of the P.S. remarks as well as the salutations, but left enough of them in to evoke his tone and style without too much redundancy. I have also attempted to edit out the more mundane passages that do not move the story along as much, but just as with the openers and closers, I feel some inclusion is necessary in order to understand the context.

Lastly, a childhood friend I shared this with put it best: my grandfather was a writer. And that's where I think all those publishers and agents who passed on the concept missed the point. The story is a common one, no doubt, but Joe tells it in a way that makes it come alive. He was an embedded reporter before there was embedded reporting. He was the real thing.

# Acknowledgments

First and foremost I'd like to thank my father, Anthony, who has always been there for me. I know he misses the Duchess more than anyone. Don Moss, my grandfather's nephew, has been tremendous in his support of the project the whole time. Thanks need to go out to Jack, Loretta, and the Shine family, the Schneider family, the Crams and the Parsons. I'd like to acknowledge my Aunt Chris, her husband Lynn, my sisters Laurel and Jill, and their husbands, Brian and Kevin. Also due thanks are Bill Evans and Jim Laris for first letting me publish the letters in the *Pasadena Weekly* way back when. Thank you to all my online friends and extended family and friends, and especially those who supported me with the campaign to bring this book back in digital form: Erin Buhl, Juliana Lyon, Ernest Rubio, Jordan Salas, Ann Erdman, Richard Gober, Lisa Emerling, Chris Davis, Laura Brusseau, Steven Vanni, Tim Root, Rae Latt, Grace Latt, Jonathan Latt, Jim Minion, Christian Fogliani, and Kim Derrick.

# 1

# An Unlikely Hero

Joseph R. Moss was actually born Joseph Robert Moscowitz in Ottawa, Canada on November 26, 1911 to Romanians David and Miriam Moscowitz. His father's profession was listed on his birth certificate as tailor, but he may have also run a small business much like a general store with groceries. David and Miriam had four other children: Eddie, Moe, Bennie, and Carrie. Joe was the youngest, the baby of the family.

Young Joe
Moss

Much of the information for this biographical sketch comes from a 1942 employment application Joe filled out. Where the application asked what his siblings did for a living, he wrote "real estate." Truth is, while they did have some real estate holdings, their real profession was running illegal gambling rackets. In other words, some of the information he provided must be taken with a grain of salt.

David Moscowitz moved his family to the United States, by way of Detroit, on April 27, 1920. Sometime around

Joey & Gertie,
Oct. 23, 1932

The family,
Circa 1935

April 1923, they moved to Los Angeles, California, where Joe would attend both grade school and high school. He graduated from Hollenbeck Junior High School in 1926 and from Roosevelt High School in 1929. He apparently attended college at Southwestern University for a year or less. He listed his major as pre-legal. On October 15, 1933, Joe Moss married his high school sweetheart, Gertrude Proto, or Gertie, in Los Angeles. Two years later on June 7, 1935, Gertie gave birth to their only child, a daughter they named Marilyn Day Moss. In his letters, Joe would only occasionally call her Marilyn, instead preferring to call her pet names he'd invented like "Slowpoke," and "the Duchess." Nicknames were a thing with Joe. Gertie often became his "Darling Chin-up Girl."

As a family, the Mosses bounced back and forth between Detroit and Los Angeles. While they lived at places like the Hotel Detroiter in Detroit, he worked for his brothers, who ran their illegal gambling rackets in the region. Eddie's son Donald Moss, who now lives in Los Angeles, recalled being shown two casinos his father ran: one in Windsor, Canada, and one in Detroit. The casino would be hidden inside a legitimate business, or a front. Don's sister, the late Teri Cram, put it this way: "These guys with small flower shops who happen to live in mansions."

Marilyn and
Uncle Eddie

Both Don and Teri said that Eddie was reluctant in his later years to discuss his gambling operations in Detroit. When Las Vegas began to boom in the late 40s, Eddie moved there and bought his own casino, the El Dorado. His brother Moe followed and worked for him.

Joe's sister Carrie married Abe Schneider, often referred to as Uncle Abe. Abe and Carrie had two boys: Burt, nicknamed Babe, and Jerry, whom Joe makes numerous references to in his letters. Uncle Abe's specialty was carnivals and amusements. When he and Carrie moved to the L.A. area, he ran some concession stands in Balboa, a part of Newport Beach, in an area that has come to be known as "the Fun Zone." When Joe, Gertie, and Marilyn went to L.A., they would spend a lot of time in Balboa. Joe worked with Abe at the booths, learning a great deal about the trade. He also conducted lessons on archery.

Joey & Jerry,
clowning around

Still, it would seem that all his life, Joe had to rely on the generosity of his older and more successful brothers, either for money, or for business and employment opportunities. It is for this reason that his relationship with his siblings, especially his brother Eddie, seemed somewhat strained. This becomes even more evident when you read his letters from boot camp. While he does correspond with them, messages coming from the brothers to Joe are few and far between.

The following letters illustrate the nature of Joe's relationship with his brothers. On January 26, 1942, Joe wrote to his brother Eddie in Detroit:

*It was quite a surprise to me to learn that you wanted to hear from me. My behavior in the past year, most certainly, was cause enough for a complete lack of interest in my welfare. I am humbly grateful to you for your inquiry. This letter, incidentally, is not by way of explaining my actions. I doubt the Good Lord above could make things clear.*

*So far, my luck has been true to form. I haven't yet found anything to do. All of my efforts have been directed towards finding employment in an airplane plant but due to the fact that I can't prove my citizenship, my application will not even be considered.*

*Truthfully, I was almost positive of gaining employment in one of the plants and as a matter of fact, I wasn't a bit worried, and now this. Then last week, I evolved the brilliant idea of looking for some sort of business—you see, I had the audacity or rather the effrontery to believe I could induce either you or Ben to set me up in business; of course, I knew what the answer would be. At least it was a good laugh.*

*At the present time, I am playing with the idea of going to either Reno or Las Vegas. I have concluded that since the only profession I know is that of gambling, and since it isn't legal anywhere except in Nevada, I may as well try my luck there.*

*The few want ads I have answered here demand experienced help, so naturally I am at a disadvantage.*

Shortly thereafter, a Western Union telegram Joe sent to Eddie on February 3, 1942: *Found downtown bar that can be handled for three thousand down. Can I interest you? If so, will write all particulars. Regards, Joe.*

Two months later, on March 14, 1942, in another letter to Eddie he wrote:

*Haven't worked since I arrived here and from the looks of things, I haven't much chance. I wrote Attorney Millstein for some official proof my citizenship, which was absolutely necessary to go to work in any defense plant. He replied with a letter stating the fact that he felt sure of my status of a citizen. The letter proved of little value to me, since the various employment people referred me to the Office of Immigration and Naturalization. Upon being interviewed there, I was told I needed a certificate of derivative citizenship. I filed the application and now I have to wait nine months for my certificate. I will try my luck in Las Vegas or Reno. If I have no luck in either of those places, I have definitely made up my mind to join some branch of the Army. Gertie, I believe, can go to work, so I won't have to worry about her and Marilyn. I know it is my only out.*

A short while after this, Joe wrote to Eddie again and explained that for five hundred dollars he could take over two of Uncle Abe's stores in the Fun Zone. Here is Eddie's one-page response:

*April 17, 1942*

*I presume Abe has mentioned our telephone conversation of a few days ago and of Ben's and my decision to send you three hundred dollars. To be very frank with you, I want to say that everything was all right with me until I found out about your two hundred dollars story to Stewart. Also, that Ben was a little peeved on learning that he had to pay Dudgy some sixty-nine dollars for you. Well, we are sending you five hundred dollars as per your letter. See if you can give us a count for this money. Trusting that this is a beginning towards a better relationship amongst us all.*

We don't know if Joe ever gave Eddie and Ben a good count for their money.

Don Moss told me that after Joe's death, his father Eddie rarely, if ever, talked about his youngest brother and would get choked up when his name was mentioned.

Now my mother had always maintained that her father had been drafted, and I decided not to belabor the point with her. My theory is that a little girl could never really accept that her father willingly left her. But based on my research, as we can see in the letter I quote from, it is possible he enlisted. Bennie's widow, Aunt Helen, when I spoke to her in 1995, suggested as much. That doesn't rule out his being drafted. Dave Marks "taking it pretty hard" suggests from the very first letter that Marks's fate wasn't of his own choosing, and perhaps so it was with Joe.

On November 15, 1943, Selective Service ordered Joe to report for induction at the local draft board in Detroit. Joe informed them that he was living Los Angeles, and they processed him there. While Joe was in the service, Gertie lived with her sister, Florence Shine, and her husband, Sam Shine, on Alfred Street in Los Angeles, along with their two young children, son Jack (referred to as Jackie in the letters) and his sister, Stephanie. Gertie went to work as a saleswoman for Saks Fifth Avenue. Meanwhile, Marilyn spent much of the time at a boarding school called Miss Ginette's.

Gertie's job provided my mother with a lot of interesting stories. One notable evening, none other than Ella Fitzgerald walked into the store to buy some gifts for her staff. Because she was black, none of the other saleswomen were willing to talk to her. My grandmother did and made a handsome commission for her efforts.

So Gertie sold lingerie to stars while Joe, once in the Army, always held out the hope that his age, thirty-three, and his status as a pre-Pearl Harbor father would keep him out of harm's way. He assured himself and his family that he would get a lucky break, such as being assigned to the Special Services branch where he could work as an entertainer, or being sent to Officer Candidate School. Meanwhile, his brothers were busy, in Joe's words, "picking horses at the track."

Joe's own inner struggle, as he grappled with the ramifications of what was happening to him, is reflected clearly in the letters. A transformation was underway, a coming of age as it were. Through his faith, love, and courage, his story honors the thousands of unknown soldiers whose stories will never be told, whose sacrifices will never be known.

# 2

# Good Soldiers

*January 3, 1944*

Well, here I am established in my barracks. We had a fairly good trip out here, although it took us three nights and two days to arrive. I feel fine, although it will be rather hard to get used to the barking of orders by the corporals and sergeants. They let you know immediately that discipline is the backbone of the Army.

Our training consists of seventeen weeks of learning how to kill; after that, only the Good Lord knows what will happen.

Dave Marks, the fellow I introduced you to in the station, is my bunkmate. That is, he has the upper and I have the lower. If you remember, I told you he was taking this quite hard and he still is. I have been trying to cheer him up and I have partly succeeded.

It was a good thing we left the station in L.A. when we did, for I think I would have broken down if we had stayed any longer. I miss you both so very much and I know that it will take a great deal of will power to concentrate on being a good soldier and keeping myself in the right frame of mind. The only bright spot is the fact that I am doing something that may contribute to the safety of my loved ones. I think I know how both you and Marilyn feel and I am sure that you, too, will be good soldiers.

Our camp is located about ten miles north of Tyler, Texas and aforementioned town is the size of an average community. If we get any overnight passes, I imagine we will spend them in Tyler. We have been told we could not get any furloughs until our seventeen weeks of basic were up.

The financial situation will not be very good, because not only are they taking twenty-two dollars for an addition to your allotment, but also I had to subscribe three dollars seventy-five cents a month for war bonds. My laundry will be one dollar fifty cents per month. Then add incidentals such as toothpaste, soap, and seven dollars thirty cents per month for insurance; I won't have much left for perhaps even cigarettes. Every corporal stationed here has a racket all his own. We had to have hangers to hang our clothes on and we had to buy them from the corporal, seven for a dollar. How do you like that?

*January 4, 1944*

Today we were taught how to make a field pack. You have seen them on soldiers in the movies. I now know how it is done. This morning also, I had my first look at German war prisoners. They all seemed cheerful and happy. The sergeant told us that most of them never want to go back to their native land and they look forward to Germany's defeat.

I had a very pleasant surprise this afternoon. As a matter of fact, I feel quite proud of myself. We are all taken to the interview department for a second questioning as to our capabilities. You recall my telling you that I had no idea what sort of score I made in my IQ at Fort MacArthur. The surprise came when the sergeant in charge read off seven names and stated that the men whose names were called were to get an additional IQ. I was one of the men and the first thing that came to my mind was that I had failed so badly in my first test that the Army could not believe anyone would receive so low a score. But much to my amazement, I was told that we were the seven highest scores out of the three hundred men in our company and our scores were so very high, that this additional test was to determine whether or not the first one was just accidental or if it showed a true picture of our intelligence. If my score this time is as high, it may mean going to Officer Candidate School (OCS). He told us that we may or may not complete our basic, depending upon the openings in the school and the war department. He also warned us not to be disappointed if we remained privates in the infantry. Well, dear, I can only say, "Blessed be those who expect the worst, verily they are never disappointed."

*January 5, 1944*

We had a rather hard day of it today. In the first place, it rained all night last night and all of today. We started the morning off by going to the drill field and lying down in the wonderful, cold, sticky, wet mud of Texas. The reason was to learn to aim a rifle. With drilling and the handling of a rifle the chief subject of the day, I'd almost forgotten calisthenics at six this morning. Everything seems so strange and it seems as though I would awaken any moment from a bad dream. But it is all real enough and one cannot help but know it when orders are barked at you and each mistake brings a barrage of profane language that makes each of us wonder how ten million before us went through all of this without committing murder.

Tonight Dave and myself went to Army Theater #4 and sat through one-third of Frank Sinatra in *Higher and Higher.* Then we went to the service club, where I wrote this letter. Writing every day isn't as simple as I thought. All I can tell you are things that occur during the day. Do I make these letters interesting? It has been very cold here mornings; as a matter of fact, it is almost eastern weather. No snow of course, but a very cold brisk wind. Not very pleasant, is it? How do all you feel? No doubt, Marilyn is quite angry with me for not writing, but tell her these letters are for both you and her. I will write her personal letters next week.

*January 6, 1944*

My Darling,
      Another full day and harder. It becomes easier to understand why we have the greatest army in the

world. Amazing as it seems, they make a first-class fighting man out of you in seventeen weeks. Most of the day was devoted to rifle drill and exercise. Sort of a hardening-up process. They insist that every recruit is in top physical condition and spare no one daily exercise.

Around five this afternoon, we were taken to the drill field to be shown a review of men who have completed their course. It was inspiring, although uncomfortable because of the extreme cold. We stood at attention for the better part of an hour. We just received our comforters today and I think we will be able to get some sleep at night. I haven't slept since our arrival because of the very cold nights. We get two army blankets, which hardly seem to keep us lukewarm. But am sure it will be all right from now on.

*January 8, 1944*

Darling,

I missed writing to you yesterday because I had been on KP from 4 a.m. to 8 p.m. last night. I have never worked as hard in my lifetime and I can assure you when I crawled to my bunk and my head hit the pillow, nothing felt as good. I couldn't possibly have written you. Today was merely a repetition of other days, with drilling and exercise and the breaking down of a rifle included.

They are giving us a break tomorrow (Sunday) by letting us sleep until 7:30 a.m.; although there are a number of things we are going to do during the afternoon, one of which will be to place all the men over twenty-eight years of age into the same

platoon and bunkhouse. This doesn't mean it will be
any easier for us. It is just the fact that one platoon
is made up of us older fellows and is called "the old
man's platoon." It will make it nice for us all, living
in the same barracks, as we will eliminate a great deal
of rowdiness—consequently, we will able to rest a
great deal more.

I finally ran into someone I knew. You remember
the chateau we had in Mt. Clemmens? There was a
nice looking, chubby fellow, whose name was Tony,
that used to work for us. I met him in the mess hall
and it was a surprise for both of us. He isn't chubby
anymore and has only two more weeks of basic training
to complete. Of course, we spoke about everyone in
Detroit that we knew.

Well, sweet, there is nothing else I can think of
so I will close thinking of you and Marilyn and will
go to sleep hoping I can dream about you. Please tell
my family not to expect any mail for at least a couple
of weeks. It will take that long for us to get into a
routine whereby we will have some free time.

All my love,
Joe

P.S. Please excuse penmanship as have been writing
on the top of my bunk.

*January 9, 1944*

I received your Sunday letter and I laughed reading
about your unfinished ironing. You certainly are
getting like Carrie. So you are getting fairly big now.
Well it's about time although I like them they way
they were. I wrote you yesterday that I was going out

on the firing range today. I didn't because I caught cold and they made me stay in my barracks. I feel much better now and your letters are the only kind of medicine I like.

More than likely, I will go out to the range tomorrow then I will write you all about it. All I did today was lie in the bunk and sweat, trying to get rid of the cold. So there isn't much news. I also received a letter from Bennie and he writes me that Dudgy went up for induction the other day and that he received a letter from Pitt, who is in Camp Berkeley, Texas, not very far from here. Ben also sent me a money order for twenty-five dollars, which I am sending to you. It's already signed; I believe Sam will cash it for you. Under no circumstances will you give the money to Abe. Please let me handle him.

Joe

P.S. Kiss the Slowpoke for me.

*January 11, 1944*

Well, I finally received your mail. I got two letters this morning and one this evening from you. I can't tell how happy they made me feel. Your picture was a pleasant surprise and as a "sister" team, both you and Flo should do very well, especially with Hawaiian costumes. Marilyn's letter was just thrilling. I can just picture her as she was writing it. Tell her to keep writing.

We had quite a few lectures today. The most important of them was the use of a gas mask. It is considered, besides the rifle, a soldier's best friend. They insist that you be very proficient in its use. Calisthenics early this morning, and then the lectures followed. I am writing this letter from the service club, where Dave and myself are now seated at a desk. We will, in all probability, finish our letters and then go back to our barracks to clean our shoes and gas masks, and then clean our mess equipment.

I haven't as of yet received your carton of cigarettes but I imagine it should be here in the next few days. I have been smoking my pipe quite a bit and I could use some of that tobacco I used to smoke, you remember? It's called Sutliff's Mixture #79. Well dear, I am going to close now. I will try to drop Lou Wish a line also. No mail as yet from Eddie or Moe, although I have written to them both since I have been here.

Nothing more.

All my love,
Joe

P.S. Kiss Marilyn for me.

*January 13, 1944*

My Darling,

No mail from you today, although I did receive a letter from Jackie. I also received a wire from Bennie asking me why he hadn't heard from me. I am going to break down and write him tonight.

We had more gas mask drill today and were also allowed to sniff various poisonous gases so as to recognize them in combat. The afternoon was spent teaching us the duties of interior guard. We were outdoors all day in a very cold drizzling rain and marched in mud up to our ankles. It is amazing that we haven't all come down with colds. The local papers state that it is the coldest it has been here in fifty-six years. We are sort of used to it now. Tonight we were all issued long winter underwear. I have mine on now and I look like a tightrope walker, but they are very warm and I know I will make good use of them.

I am anxiously awaiting the woolen socks. With all the marching we do, they would certainly be a godsend. I imagine they should be here in the next few days.

*January 14, 1944*

My Darling,

No mail from you today either, but I imagine it's being held up. I received a letter from our swell daughter, though, and I am very proud of the manner in which she writes. I am happy, too, in the fact that she thinks of her daddy.

Today was much the same as the preceding days, except that we did our exercise in a blinding snowstorm. It has been snowing here since early last night and I can't say I like it very much. We were taught the different positions of holding a rifle while shooting on a range this afternoon, and were also shown a picture of the results of venereal diseases. Very disgusting, and we had to eat chow immediately afterwards.

This letter will have to be short also, as we have a complete inspection of all our equipment tomorrow morning and I will have to get to work cleaning everything up. I will have time to write everyone this Sunday, so tell them not to be angry with me. We haven't much time to ourselves and I am fortunate in being able to write you every day.

Nothing more. I love you very much and miss the both of you something fiercely.

As always yours,<br>Joe

P.S. Tell Jackie and Marilyn I will answer them Sunday also. I love you.

*January 15, 1944*

My Darling,

Received two letters from you, as well as a letter from Marilyn and the box with my sox and handkerchiefs. In both your letters, you ask me to write everyday. I haven't missed one day, outside of last Sunday writing to you, dear. Our mail here does not go out every day and if it does, it is sometimes held up in Dallas. You will notice that I do not use airmail; ordinary mail from here will arrive in L.A. in approximately the same time as airmail.

More lectures today, one on map reading, and another on the cause we are fighting for. We marched through mushy, sloppy snow carrying a rifle and we were certainly tired at the end of the day. A great many of the boys received overnight passes and went to Tyler, which is about ten miles from here. I could have gone also, but I would have had to sleep on the floor of the USO. So I am staying in camp. Dave and myself may go into town tomorrow just to see what the town looks like and also to try and get ourselves a steak dinner. You have the opinion, I imagine, that the reason for the civilian shortage of steaks was because all the meat was going to the Army. I haven't seen anything that looks like a steak since I've been here.

It tickles me to read about Marilyn's sudden interest in getting to school on time. I suppose her teacher must have sent home a strong note. How is she getting along with the piano? I forgot to mention that I received a letter from Moe today. He has just gotten back into action and feels fine now. He asked about you and Marilyn and hoped you were both fine. His writing indicates that even his letters are done in a hurry.

Well, we can sleep until 7:30 a.m. tomorrow morning, which is a pleasure to think about. I certainly am going to take advantage of it. There isn't much else I can write, my sweet, so will close loving you and missing you. Keep right on with the same kind of letters, I can't tell you how much they mean to me.

*January 16, 1944*

My Darling,

No mail from you today, but I suppose I will have two tomorrow. We slept late today—7:30—had chow and then went to Kilgore, Texas, about twenty-five miles from here. We had a steak at the Kilgore Hotel, then walked around most of the afternoon, came back and took a shower, washed most of my clothes, then came up to the service club to write letters. I have just written to Eddie, Bennie, and Moe. My hand is about ready to drop off.

Tomorrow starts another week of basic. It will get tougher as we go along, so I understand. At any rate, it will bring me one more week closer to you. Sunday is the hardest day to take. Other days during the week, I am occupied so I don't feel the distance as much.

I love you so.

Joe

P.S. Am writing to Marilyn also.

*January 17, 1944*

My Darling,

I knew I would receive two letters from you today. I did. Also a letter from Marilyn. More lectures and drill today and each day that passes, they give it to us a little bit tougher.

We were taught how to tell where we are on a map and also taught to read a compass. Then we were lectured on windage and elevation in firing a rifle. We are to have two weeks of range firing with real bullets starting next week. It is now 7:20 p.m. and we are all waiting to be interviewed by the second lieutenant of our company. He will probably ask how we like army life and how it is affecting us. It is purely a formality they always go through.

You keep asking when I am to take my second IQ. I took it the same day I wrote you about it. I will not be told my score until the end of my basic and at that time if my score is high enough and if there is an opening in the OCS, I may be sent to it. On the other hand, I may be sent to the signal corps or the quartermaster corps and then again, I may just stay in the infantry. I just have to be lucky.

P.S. In case I frequently forget to send regards to everyone, you know it is just an oversight. Kiss Marilyn for me. Tell her I received her letter and will try to answer her at least by Sunday.

*January 18, 1944*

Your Saturday's letter arrived this morning and Sunday's this afternoon. Your letters are swell, honey, and make me feel as though I were there with you. I also received a letter from Marilyn, which was very cute. She has been telling me what she has for dinner and I get a big laugh out of them.

It's a pity about Fay's brother, but those are the fortunes of war. Today was practically a repetition of other days, except that we were taught first aid on the battlefield. We were also shown movies on booby traps, which were quite interesting. We had more drill this afternoon and then marched for about five miles with a combat pack and our rifles. I was ready to drop at the end of the march. I am very tired and as a matter of fact, I am already undressed and sitting in my bunk writing this letter, and it is only 8:30.

Dave received a salami from his mother in Chicago; the trouble is we haven't any rye bread or any kind of bread to eat it with.

P.S. Kiss Marilyn for me.

*January 19, 1944*

My Darling,
Today, we were on the drill field all day, practicing different positions in firing a rifle. It was pretty

strenuous and getting into the positions are very uncomfortable and unnatural, but the Army claims you can be a sharpshooter using them.

After night chow, we were given the "pleasant" news that we were to have a general inspection of the company area, which meant that we had to give our barracks a real going-over, besides cleaning the outside of our area. Believe me, I am writing this letter on my nerve only. Outside of all I have written, we had a fine day. Incidentally, the weather here has turned swell and it is almost like California weather. There isn't a trace of snow.

*January 21, 1944*

My Darling,

Received two letters and the tobacco today. The tobacco got here just in time. I have been using Dave's and he ran short today. Thank you very much, sweet, I appreciate it no end. I can see by your letters that you are quite busy on Marilyn's coat. I know it will be nothing short of beautiful when you are finished.

Today was one of those tough days. We started out as usual with our exercises, and then continued them with a nine-pound rifle. After a few moments, you would swear the rifle weighed one hundred nine pounds. Then we made up the full field packs, which weigh in the neighborhood of sixty pounds, and put them on our backs, and also carried our rifles and wore a three-pound steel helmet.

We then took a short jaunt of five miles through the woods. A very enjoyable day!

Tomorrow is Inspection Day again. Everything

is to be spic and span and I had to get a haircut. I haven't any left now. Hair, I mean.

P.S. My kiss for Marilyn and one for you, too. I guess I don't have to say more. Have you heard from Jerry? Received a letter from Moe, he is back in action, or maybe I have already told you. Regards to everyone. Am anxiously awaiting the strudel. Could go for some of those cookies of yours, too.

*January 22, 1944*

Well, sweet, this has been the hardest of days so far. We have been on our feet since six this morning without a letup. They tell you that the infantry is made up of foot soldiers and it was, by all means, proven to me today. I can't remember when I have ever been so tired. We started as usual with physical training and then map reading, bayonet practice, field drill, and for dessert, marching in time to music.

I am writing this letter from the service club. We finally got a little time off. Dave and myself were going to go into Tyler tonight and we bought our bus tickets and signed out. Then we went to the bus stop and waited for a bus. There seemed to be around a thousand fellows also waiting, so we decided to give it up and come back to the service club to write our letters. We are going to the show after we are done. The picture is Robert Taylor in *Song of Russia*. Imagine it is quite new.

*January 23, 1944*

My Darling,

Dave and myself finally got to Tyler today. Just had a steak dinner at the Blackstone Hotel and enjoyed it. We are now in the local USO, and I am very surprised at its size. They have just about every thing in here. The only bad features are the fact that servicemen have to pay for their food here.

I received another letter from Marilyn, which was very cute. She tries to be so interesting and grown up. She also sent me a drawing of herself.

P.S. Kiss the Slowpoke.

*January 24, 1944*

Received two letters from you today. You most certainly are a busy girl, but I know you love it. We were mighty busy today also with getting ourselves ready to go out onto the firing range. They are very insistent that everyone learns to shoot a rifle and they won't take *no* for an answer. This afternoon we went on a forced march, without any equipment. A forced march is one in which you travel about five miles per hour. We hiked three miles. I was so tired that I was in bed right after chow and as soon as I finish this letter, I am going to sleep.

*January 25, 1944*

My Darling,

I received your letter dated Saturday and I also received your strudel. Boy, how good it is! Dave and myself dug into the box and Dave says it tastes just like his mother's! I also received a very cute letter from Marilyn. She included a knitted patch to show me the kind of knitting she is doing.

*January 28, 1944*

A letter from both you and Marilyn and my slippers. Gosh, how swell they feel! Received a letter also from Johnny Belda. Do you remember him? He used to work for us on Cuss Avenue as a ticket writer. We called him "Little Johnny." He is in the Army Air Forces Ground Crew, is doing very well, and asked to be remembered.

Finally, I got onto the firing range today. My cold is gone and although I was still a bit weak, shot a fair score for a beginner. On my first shot, the rifle wasn't set into my shoulder and the kick of the shell brought the base of the rifle on my eye, so I am now sporting a pretty shiner. I had to shoot a great deal to catch up with other fellows and it sort of tired me out. Got back in about 6 p.m. and then had our mail call, in which I received the mail I have already mentioned.

I can imagine how well Al Lewis liked your dinner. It makes me feel swell, too, seeing that you are nice to him. He is a fine fellow. You don't have to hurry with the socks now, dear. I found an army store in Tyler that sells them and I have enough now to last me a while. Really would appreciate a great big box of your fudge, can you manage?

*January 29, 1944*

In reading your letter, I burst out laughing at the paragraph that you told of making fudge for me, as in yesterday's letter to you I asked if it were possible for you to make some to send me. Just shows you that our minds are in perfect harmony. I sure will appreciate it when it gets here and I will probably ration it to myself to one piece a night.

*January 30, 1944*

We had another tough day today. It rained all of the time we were out on the range. I don't think I told you that we have been eating our noon chow on the range and we ate it today in a driving rainstorm without any kind of shelter. Our food kept floating around the mess kits and it was quite a trick trying to spear something to eat.

*January 31, 1944*

My Darling,

Yours and Marilyn's letters today. Glad both of you are well. I don't blame everyone for wanting your piecrusts and other bakeries; your strudel was the greatest success ever here.

On the range again today, only from today until Thursday, all of our scores will be recorded and become official. We are firing now to determine whether or not we can get one of three different types of medals. My score today was very low and I imagine I will be lucky to qualify as an ordinary rifleman. It doesn't mean very much, because regardless how badly you shoot, you cannot get out of the infantry.

There is a rumor around camp that ours will be the last cycle to go through here; after our basic, they are going to close the camp. I feel that the rumor is a true one because since our arrival, there haven't been any new trainers shipped here. See how lucky I am. If this could only have come a couple of months ago, I might have been sent to Camp Roberts.

*February 1, 1944*

My Darling,

No mail from you, probably two tomorrow. Feeling pretty good since I got over my cold and it's amazing how quickly I recovered. My resistance must be getting to a rather high pitch. After writing you last night, they called us out to receive our pay. I got the grand sum of six dollars ten cents, which isn't too bad for a month's work. Well, that's my first pay from the Army and I suppose it won't be the last. On the range again today. My firing was a little better, though I am still far from being a good shot.

*February 4, 1944*

My Darling,

Received a letter today. Glad the money order came in time. I know you can make use of it. We had a thorough inspection for two hours this morning and followed up with two hours of drill. This afternoon we went on a four-hour march, carrying a full field pack. You can't fathom how tired I am right now. It is sheer will power that keeps my pen in my hand.

But they want to get us into condition and that is their method. It really is amazing what they can do with you. Our rifles weigh in the neighborhood of nine pounds and I now can handle it like a toothpick. Slowly but surely they are molding us into a combat outfit.

Well, sweet, I cannot go any farther. I really am tired and can just about keep my eyes open so until tomorrow I am closing. I love you very much.

Yours,<br>Joe

P.S. Kiss the Slowpoke for me.

*February 5, 1944*

My Darling,

A letter from you today. Each time you tell me you are sending a package, I can hardly wait until it gets here. I believe I have told you before that we cannot get a thing here and the aftershave lotion is really a godsend. Of course, I haven't received it as yet, but I imagine it will be here soon.

Today we had quite a number of different subjects, mainly a review of the things we have already been taught. We received another shot in the arm this morning. I don't know what this one is supposed to prevent but at any rate, we are to get around fifteen different kinds. In the afternoon, we were taken to the five hundred-yard rifle range and we were taught the technique of rifle fire. In other words, we were taught how to get the most effect in firing upon the enemy.

*February 7, 1944*

We threw our hand grenades today and it wasn't as exciting as I thought it would be. All there is is the expectancy of the explosion. It sounds like a giant firecracker. The grenade is one of our best offensive weapons and they certainly spend a great deal of time showing us the best methods of using it. This afternoon, we had more first aid and then went through four of the deadliest kinds of gases. With our gas masks on, we went through a gas chamber full of tear gas.

*February 12, 1944*

My Darling,

No doubt you have been wondering why you haven't heard from me. Honey, they have had us going at the top speed since Wednesday. I not only haven't had anytime to write but even if I did have, I couldn't have held a pen in my hand, I was that tired. I have received each of your letters since, though, and I also received the box of candied nuts.

They certainly were delicious. I laughed so at your note, too. I showed it to the fellows and they all got quite a kick out of it.

We have been doing a great deal of firing and quite a bit of drilling. This afternoon, they marched us three miles with a full field pack and rifle at one hundred seventy steps a minute. Most of the men in our platoon dropped out at the halfway mark. I made it on my nerve only, because I can assure you my legs were gone also at the halfway mark. Dave made the complete march with me and we both said we wouldn't do it again. That is, we would drop out when we couldn't go any further. Four of the fellows that went the complete distance passed completely out at the end, so you can imagine how tough it was.

*February 14, 1944*

Another very rough day today. We started the day by going out to the drill field for a class on a firearm called a mortar; it's a sort of cross between a small cannon and a rocket gun. A very powerful weapon and quite complicated. Then this afternoon, we had to run what is known as bayonet assault course, and honey, if I have said that the past few weeks were tough, I've been mistaken. The bayonet course is the hardest thing I have ever done. It is a course laid out for one-half mile with all kinds of hazards, including six-foot walls, four-foot ditches that have to be jumped, and an eight-foot deep and twenty-foot wide ditch that has to be crossed by running across a log. Then along the way are numerous dummies that have to be bayoneted correctly. This is all done at a dead run. I ran the course three times; of course, I mean I ran it the first time and walked it the next two times. I'm not tired because there just isn't any sense of feeling left. But it had to be done and I am glad it is over with.

*February 15, 1944*

My Darling,
　　Received a letter from you and Marilyn, also the box of cookies. I don't have to tell you how delicious

they are. You say that I sounded depressed in my last letter. I am sorry, honey, that I gave you that impression. Naturally, I am not happy. I miss you and Marilyn so much that it hurts, but I am trying to make the best of it. If my letters sound depressing, just ignore it because I am not in that mood at all.

I don't know whether or not you read the letter the Slowpoke wrote me, but in the event that you haven't, I am enclosing it because I am sure it will make you "swell" as I have. She is so very clever that at times she amazes me.

We marched five miles today out to a new rifle range and fired at what is known as transition firing. It means that we fire at targets that are placed at different distances and fire at them rapidly. I did quite well.

It was a long march back, sweet, and I am very tired so I'll close until tomorrow.

I love you always,
Joe

P.S. Thanks again for the cookies and please don't forget the razor and at least a dozen of those snapshots I mentioned. I need the pictures for a special reason.

*The letter from Marilyn:*

*Sun. 13, 1944*

Dearest Daddy,
   I am very sorry I didn't write to you. I didn't because I didn't have any envelopes in school.

I received the valentine you sent me and thanks a lot. I hope you received Mother's and mine.

I went to the show and I saw *Springtime in the Rockies* and *This Thing Called Love*. It was the second time I saw it.

I have a lot of fun at Miss Ginette's school. We get to listen to the radio almost every night.

Mother is giving me a fifty-cent-a-week allowance. I am very happy about it.

Miss Ginette is going to let all the girls in the front house have a garden of their own, and I sleep in the front house.

Friday night I was putting my cloths on the bed. I wanted everything to be as neat as a pin. The biggest girl there said I was busiest girl there.

Well sweetheart, I miss you a lot and I wish they had not of taken you in. But I know that every father has to do his part in this war. I am buying war stamps. I haven't any more to say but closing with all my love.

> Your loving daughter and
> pal,
> Marilyn

*February 17, 1944*

My Darling,

Missed writing you yesterday although I did receive your letter. Also received one from Moe in which he told me he was writing you in answer to yours.

It has been raining constantly and we have been in mud up to our knees every day. It is hard enough to march when it is dry but when it rains, it is a very great effort. I can't seem to get enough sleep and I have been so tired that sometimes I have gone to sleep standing up.

We are making a great deal of progress, something new each day. We spent the morning working with mortars and the afternoon we were learning the offensive tactics of the infantryman. Crawling through mud and running at top speed in a half-crouch were some of the lessons learned. This, of course, is all done while carrying our combat packs and rifle.

*February 19, 1944*

I didn't write you yesterday because we had to prepare for a rigid all-afternoon inspection and we had to use every minute of the evening. Yesterday we were out in a training combat zone area digging more foxholes, only after they were dug we had to crouch over in them and then a light tank ran over the hole. It was quite a thrill, wondering whether the tread of a sixty-ton tank would come crashing down upon us, but all of us came through in fine shape. It is still raining and four or five inches of caked mud on our feet is getting to be quite the thing. We don't mind it anymore.

Dave and myself are here at the USO just trying to get away from camp for a while. They are having a dance here, so as usual, we will sit around smoking our pipes and watching the youngsters go to it.

# 3

# There's No Business Like Show Business

*February 21, 1944*

I hit the jackpot today. Two letters from you, a box of strudel and cookies from your mother, and two boxes of cookies from the Showmen's.

I didn't write to you yesterday because I was a pretty busy little boy. The first time I visited the Tyler USO, I told the director that if at any time I could be of any help in her variety shows on Sunday nights, I would be glad to help out. So she was stuck for a show last night and asked me if I could put one on. So Dave and I were double MCs and we put the show on. We had a lot of fun and everyone seemed to like us. There was a quartet from camp and also a girl's trio. Dave and I did a few blackouts that were quite successful. At any rate, we kept them laughing and no one walked out, so it gives you some idea of how we sold our stuff. Of course, there wasn't any remuneration and we got quite a big kick out of it ourselves.

It has finally stopped raining although we are still wallowing in mud. Well, my darling, nothing much else so am closing. Am very tired and the bed is so inviting. 'Till tomorrow,

I love you.<br>Joe

P.S. Kiss the Slowpoke. Thank your mother for me.

*February 22, 1944*

My Darling,

Today, your birthday, and the second month of my Army career. Many, many happy returns of the day, my sweetheart. I have forgotten just how old you are, conveniently of course.

Started to rain again very early and we were out on the field all day. Mud and water, cold and wet, but they stop for nothing. Had an all-morning class in Army hygiene and how to make the most use of anything we may find while in a combat area. Then followed a written test (also in the rain) on map reading.

The afternoon was devoted to mortar instruction and following that, a four-mile forced march at a pace of one hundred sixty steps a minute. I didn't complete the march, as my legs just couldn't take it. I wasn't by myself, most of the fellows in our platoon dropped out one by one. Got back to the barracks about 5:30 p.m., had chow, and then cleaned our rifles. Around 8:00 p.m., Dave and I decided to walk to the service club. I am writing this letter from the club now.

Nothing more, dear, so am closing. Have dreamt about you and Marilyn for the past three nights, so I kind of look forward to going to sleep.

I love you,<br>Joe

P.S. Regards to everyone. Kiss the Slowpoke.

*February 24, 1944*

My Darling,

We have been out in the combat area for the past two days firing mortars. It is quite interesting and very amazing how we can hit a target beyond a hill without even seeing the target. Got back to the barracks to find that they had taken out all of the double bunks and make single ones out of them. It sure will seem funny sleeping so close to the floor again.

Dave and myself are at the service club now writing letters. A big dance is now in session and the jitterbugs are going full blast.

I am so proud of the Slowpoke and each line you write about her makes me wonder how she does the things you tell me.

Till tomorrow,<br>I love you.<br>Joe

*February 26, 1944*

My Darling,

Saturday night and here I am at the service club trying to write you as long a letter as possible, for this will have to do for yesterday's and today's. I sort of hit the jackpot again today, letters from you and Marilyn, and a letter from Stewart Siegel, who is now in the Army and also stationed at Camp Roberts.

Almost forgot to mention I also received a letter from Carrie also, sure tickled me. I am going to try catch up with all my mail tomorrow. Marilyn's was as sweet a letter as she has ever written and it seems she is determined to become a pianist. I sure hope so.

P.S. Kiss the Slowpoke!

*February 29, 1944*

My Darling,

Again, one letter will have to take the place of two. Had one of those tough days yesterday and after getting back from late chow, I went right to bed. In today's mail, there were two letters from you and a very wonderful letter from the Slowpoke. I just sat there and read it over and over. Besides signing her letters in this manner "From your loving daughter and pal," she now inserts a great many "honeys" in her sentences. Cute, eh?

I am sorry I didn't go into detail about our show; yes, we did quite a few of those blackouts I used to discuss with you, including a few new ones that were quite successful. I wish you could have seen the show, dear. I know you would have gotten quite a kick out of it.

Another rough day and I am ready for bed again. Out on a combat range all day, creeping, crawling, and running, falling, and firing our rifles at German dummies.

*March 3, 1944*

My Darling,

We were out in the field all morning reviewing everything we learned about mortars. The weather turned very cold all of a sudden and that sweater will be mighty handy. As I look around the barracks, I see everyone writing letters. It is so very seldom that we have any free time after noon chow that we are all trying to take advantage of it.

Am glad you are going to the department you like, dear. I know you will be much more satisfied. How is the Slowpoke getting along with her piano? Is she learning to speak French? Received a letter from Babe yesterday. Tell him I will answer as soon as I can.

*March 4, 1944*

My Darling,

Don't know whether or not there is any mail from you, as I left camp to go to Tyler about noon. I have been trying to get my certificate of derivative citizenship and the Department of Justice wrote me that they had it in Tyler, so they called the company commander and asked him to give me permission to be at their office in Tyler this afternoon. I took the oath of allegiance and they gave me the certificate, not only that but I have the afternoon off. Here I am in the USO writing to you. I will have to keep the certificate until after my basic, as in case there is any chance of my going to OCS I will need it. In the meantime, here is the number of the certificate. Make several copies of it so that in the event I lose the original, I can get a duplicate immediately.

Love,
Joe

P.S. Kiss the Slowpoke.

*March 4, 1944*

My Darling,

This is my third letter today; it's a novelty my being able to write so many times. I received the package today and each and every thing was wonderful. Honey, you look absolutely beautiful in your picture. I showed it to all the boys and every one of them whistled, which is a great compliment in the Army. Your fudge is delicious. I am hoarding it this time. Please thank Carrie for the shaving soap; it's swell, but I have no use for it—you see, I haven't much time to shave, as I have to use soap in a tube.

Made us tramp around in the mud for four hours. We have a fourteen-mile march scheduled for tomorrow afternoon, so I think I had better get to bed and get some sleep.

*March 7, 1944*

My Darling,

No mail today. Imagine it is the usual red tape in delivery. Looking for one tomorrow. We were out on the machine gun combat range all day. Worked in groups and shot at surprise targets. Pretty tiring work, for it is necessary to carry the machine gun at a crouch for quite a distance and then we had to creep and crawl with them. The march back to the barracks was very hard and I sure was glad to hit the bunk.

Had the sun out all day, but it was very cold with it. I have been wearing my longies and I now can appreciate the warmth yours used to give you in Detroit, remember?

Just eight weeks to go after this one and believe me, I have never wanted time to pass so quickly. It seems as though I have been here for a year.

Just got through cleaning the machine guns we used today, and Dave and I are sitting here at the service club writing. We are going to the camp theatre to watch *See Here, Private Hargrove*. We certainly should be able to pick out any mistakes in the picture now.

*March 8, 1944*

Dave and I were called into the Special Services office tonight and it looks as though we are both cast for a part in an all-camp show called *Strip for Action*. It was a recent New York hit and sounds very good. I have the part of Joey, a burlesque comic, so far. Of course, they may change the cast around, so nothing is definite.

*March 9, 1944*

My Darling,

A letter from you today and am very happy that everyone is feeling fine. So you are back in your old department. I know you will not regret making the change. Here it is twelve midnight and we have just gotten back from a night problem; they had hot tomato soup waiting for us and it sure tastes good. After floundering around in the woods and in complete darkness for four hours, it sure seems nice to get to our barracks.

*March 11, 1944*

Received two of your letters yesterday, although I couldn't write to you. Just had enough time to shower and get to bed. Spent the entire evening cleaning all of my equipment so that I would be ready for a general inspection this morning. I passed inspection and by virtue of this fact, I was able to come to Tyler tonight.

Just mailed you the package I mentioned; it contains a GI razor, my fountain pen medal, and a very cute picture frame for which I wanted those snapshots. I sent the pen to you because the Michigan Showmen's sent me a very beautiful new Schaeffer Skyline pen. Very thoughtful of them, wasn't it?

One of those very rough days. I am more than happy it is over. We were on the bayonet assault course and had to run it twice. Then they took squads of twelve men each and we picked up a young tree and had to throw it around as though it were a toothpick. I was all whacked out by the end of the day.

I told you that Dave and I were tentatively cast in the all-camp show, and we received the schedule of rehearsals today, so it looks as though we are in it. We may get lucky enough to get a real break with it. When I say all-camp show, I mean that it isn't a show given for just our company, but the cast is picked from the thousands of men here and given to everyone in camp. The last all-camp show was a musical and was such a tremendous hit that it played the outlying towns for quite a while for bond selling purposes. If this show sticks, we may do the same thing and may even go further! At any rate, the lieutenant in charge told me that the breaks are on our side and I may be able to do myself a great deal of good. I sure hope so. I would like to get into the Special Service Division after my basic. It is the nicest unit in the Army.

*March 13, 1944*

You say you could stand a bit of my romancing—gosh, what do you think I have been longing for all these weeks? I go to bed thinking of you and get up thinking of you. That thing of mine is getting rusty. I keep remembering the things we used to do and how wonderful it was to be with you. I have been a very good boy and my thoughts are of you only. Well, the days are going fairly fast, so get the "derby" ready, honey. I'll be home soon.

P.S. Marilyn says she isn't slow anymore, so she doesn't want me to call her Slowpoke. Kiss her for me and think of me the night you receive this letter, that is, when you get to bed. I'll try some thought transference. Perhaps we can reach each other through the thought waves. It's silly, but let's try.

*March 14, 1944*

Just got back from rehearsal and am just a bit tired. We didn't actually rehearse; it was more a reading of the show.

The character I portray is a burlesque comedian who comes to Camp Fannin to help his buddy, who is in the Army, to put on a burlesque show for the soldiers. There are many funny situations and I think the boys here are going to get a great kick out of it!

Received your letter yesterday and didn't have any time to answer it. Just came back from breakfast chow and still have a little time before we move out, so I am writing you now.

Had some instruction on the rocket gear yesterday and he gave us some more movies on booby traps. Physical training was part of the curriculum, of course, and a speed march last night, which I fortunately missed because of the rehearsal. They are supposed to issue scripts of the show tonight and if I landed the part I wrote you about, why, I will get a script. I have to do my first session of guard duty tonight. We go on at 6 p.m. and walk guard until 6 a.m. That is we are on two hours and off four. Started to rain again yesterday and it is just raining hard enough to make it good and muddy. I would sure appreciate some sunshine.

Joe

P.S. Kiss the Slowpoke. How is my sweater coming along? Dear, when you send it, send me my brown shoes along with it. I sure could use them. I forgot to tell you. I was supposed to file an income tax return. It is a little late now but it can be done. You will find all of my check stubs from the Longo Parlor in the black ledger. Can you have it made out for me? I think you will have to send me the form so I can sign it.

P.S. Kiss the Slowpoke. Regards.

*March 17, 1944*

Received very disappointing news from the Service Department. The general of the post read the script

*Strip for Action* and decided it wasn't fit for the soldiers. He wants something to show the glory of the infantry, so they have to write a complete new show. Now we will have to wait until the new one is written. Too bad because the show was all cast and we were already into it pretty well.

They gave us all morning to get ready for another general inspection, which we had this afternoon. Then this evening, we had our first Regimental Retreat parade. I never walked so much in my life and I am tired.

P.S. Kiss the Slowpoke and please tell her to write me. Can you spare fifteen dollars? If you can't, never mind. I sure can use it.

*The letter to the Slowpoke:*

Dearest Slowpoke,

I have been very busy learning to be a good soldier and I study very hard. A person has to keep on practicing and studying to be very good in anything they do and I know you want to be a real pianist, so you will have to keep on practicing every day. Study real hard, sweetheart; it won't be very long before you will be able to play any song I ask you to.

Nothing else to write you, dear, so I'll close missing you and mother very much and loving you both lots and lots.

Always,
Daddy

*March 19, 1944*

I haven't heard anything from Special Services as yet, but am still hoping.

Marilyn's letter was as cute as always. She still signs her letters "your loving daughter and pal." Do I get a big kick out of that! She enclosed one of the spelling papers and wanted me to see that she received 100% for her effort.

Al mentioned the fact that he was taking you out; I imagine he wanted to make sure I wouldn't become the irate husband.

# 4

# Christening
# the Duchess

*March 21, 1944*

First day of spring, sure doesn't look like it here. A very
cold rain is beating down making us feel as desolate
as the weather. The only bright spot of the day was
yours and Marilyn's letters. Marilyn's was especially
cute today; she asked me pleadingly not to call her
Slowpoke anymore, so I won't!

The march last night practically knocked us out.
All of us had sore feet and were more than glad to crawl
into our bunks. They didn't awaken us until 10 a.m.
That really was appreciated. We had a comparatively
easy day. They took a picture of the whole company
while the sun came out for a second. I'll send you one
as soon as they are ready. Then for the last hour of the
afternoon, we had a lecture on "Why We Fight." The
speaker was very interesting and brought home a few
good points. I am waiting for chow call now and I am

going to give myself a break after chow and go into Tyler. Feel like seeing some civilians.

P.S. Am sending the "Duchess" two stamps for her album. Kiss her for me.

*As far as one can tell this was the first time, in his letters at least, that Joe dubbed my mother the "Duchess," perhaps out of respect for her tenacity in insisting she no longer be called "Slowpoke." A duchess, of course, is a woman either married to or in the same standing as a duke.*

*March 23, 1944*

My Darling,

I missed writing to you yesterday so this one will have to do for both days. Yours and Marilyn's letters at hand, and the Duchess's was especially cute. She apologized for the briefness of her letter and her apology was so grown up. Had to clean a few automatic rifles last night and that's the reason I didn't write. We were on the range all day in another driving rain. Very uncomfortable, soaked into the bone, but we kept on firing. Had a comparatively easy day today, outside of a forced march this morning. We marched five miles in forty minutes. Then this evening, we have retreat parade in front of the general. He said we looked very good.

*March 25, 1944*

My Darling,

Your very swell letter today. Am glad you received the package. I knew you would like the picture frame.

Am going to send you another for the Duchess. Of course, you can wear the medal at any time. Here it is Saturday night and I have just taken a shower. Had another tough day today. We were out on the combat range today, learning how combat pistols work. Waded through swamps and quicksand. I was black from head to toe and couldn't wait until I got into a shower. It is surprising how much punishment the human body can take and I believe I took plenty today. But in spite of it all, I feel swell physically.

*March 26, 1944*

Your letter today containing the check. I don't know how to thank you, because I was flat and payday is a long ways off. I won't make a habit out of asking you for money. It was swell of you to send it. Going to the show tonight, to see a musical. We never go if they show any picture that deals with war.

*March 27, 1944*

Your letter of Sunday received. Hope you got to Carrie's in time for breakfast. Sure was tickled about the Duchess getting up so early and getting on the piano. I sincerely believe she will eventually become a very good pianist and there's no telling how far she will go.

We were out on the combat range all day again. Very tiring and strenuous. We have two all-night problems this week, which I know will not be any picnic. In the event I miss writing you, you will know why. I believe I told you that our bivouac officially starts on April 17.

*March 30, 1944*

My Darling,

Yesterday we were on a combat range and then there followed an eight-hour night problem. We didn't get in until 4 a.m., had breakfast, and slept until noon.

I know what it means to be lonesome, sweet, and I am rather glad you had that cry. It should relieve you somewhat. I wish I could do that same thing. It won't be very much longer now. Just a matter of five more weeks.

In today's letter, you wrote of a pet sparrow that hadn't shown up. It is the first I have heard about it. Apparently, one of your letters hasn't arrived as yet, in which the sparrow is mentioned. The letter was probably sent back for postage due, since the increase in the postal rates. Received a letter from Jackie from Murrieta Hot Springs. I laughed so heartily when he enclosed regulation sergeant stripes. He imagines those kinds of promotions come very easily.

I too was very proud of the song the Duchess wrote. She seems to have a flair for synonyms and antonyms. Her cadence is very good too, and certainly can be developed.

Nothing much else, so am closing for now. Another night problem Friday, so I'd better get some sleep. Till tomorrow,

Regards to everyone. Hope your cold is better.

*April 1, 1944*

Well, we got in early this morning after a hectic all-night problem, in which absolutely nothing was accomplished. I sincerely believe they had nothing else for us to do today, and a night problem looked very good on paper.

All we did was lose sleep and we naturally had no chance of sleeping in the foxholes. They were so uncomfortable; we couldn't even sit in them.

I wrote my last letter to you from the camp service club, and after mailing, I sat in the club listening to the regimental orchestra. I was sitting there thinking of you and trying to recall all of the fun we had and my thoughts carried me back to the days before we were married. I was trying to think of the name of our special song when all of a sudden, the band started to play it—you know, *The Hour of Parting*. I came to with a start, believe me. I didn't stay to hear the whole number because somehow or other it didn't seem right, hearing it without you in my arms. I guess I had a few tears in my eyes when I left. Shameful isn't it? A big boy like me.

> Yours,
> Joe

P.S. Kiss the Duchess for me. Regards. Haven't heard from my brothers in over a month.

*April 4, 1944*

My Darling,

Missed writing you again yesterday, we had an all-night march last night and had to prepare for it. We rested most of the day yesterday except for a few written tests we had to take. I slept most of the day and by the time I was ready to write you, they told us to get ready for the march. We marched a total of twenty miles in seven hours and fifteen minutes. Got

back to the barracks at 4 a.m. and fell asleep immediately upon hitting the pillow. They woke us at 11
a.m. and we had our mail call, in which I received
your letter and letters from Moe and his Showmen's
Club. We cleaned our equipment until four and
then dressed in our Class A uniforms for a Regimental Retreat parade. We had chow after that and now
Dave and I are at the service club writing.

Moe asked about you and Marilyn and wondered
why you haven't answered his letter. He said that it
looks as though Bennie is going to open both spots at
the park. Moe is doing OK. Says that Eddie's elbow is
still in a cast and that is why he hasn't written me.

As far as I know, sweet, we will get a furlough
after our basic is over. But in the Army, we can never
be sure of anything. I will know more about it after
our bivouac is over. We come off of bivouac April
30 and then we have one week of post-cycle work.
At that time, we will be classified and given our furloughs. So we can only hope and pray.

I meant to tell you, dear, if you send me any
packages while we are on bivouac, don't insure them
and make them small. Otherwise, they will hold until
we get back to camp.

P.S. Sure got a kick out of the antics of the Duchess.
Am very, *very* proud of her. Don't like the idea of you
losing weight. Please take care of yourself.

*April 6, 1944*

My Darling,

Haven't had much opportunity to do anything
except work, sleep, and eat. Consequently, there isn't

much I can tell you. The problems at night are more of a nuisance value than anything else—just something to make us a bit more miserable—but there is only a short while to go now. We are in the "stretch." I can't tell you how anxious I am to reach the end of these five weeks. I keep thinking about you and Marilyn, realizing that each hour that passes brings me that much closer to you.

*April 7, 1944*

Your letter and a big beautiful box of See's candy yesterday. You don't know how much I appreciate it. Had another night problem last night and they tell us we are to have five of them next week.

Our night work hasn't been too bad, because we have had a swell break in the weather.

Nothing much has happened, keeping our noses to the grindstone. All of the fellows have one thing in mind and that is our furloughs after basic is over; believe me we think of nothing else. Four short weeks left. Monday we are to get another physical examination to see whether or not we are fit enough to go bivouac. Was at the dental clinic yesterday morning and they drilled and filled four teeth in half an hour. Also took impressions for my partial plates. They will be ready in a few days. I will be able to chew on your swell steaks when I get home.

*April 8, 1944*

My Darling,

I, too, wished that we could all have been together last night. Dave and myself went to the home of Mr.

& Mrs. Schoffman. They are a young modern couple and have two fine children. A very pretty home that was inviting as any modern home could be. A very beautiful table setting and we were served by two colored maids, one of which does all the Jewish cooking for Mrs. Schoffman. The food was delicious and believe it or not, I had two pieces of gefilte fish. I can't tell you how wonderful it made me feel to be able to sit in the front room of a home again. Each time I looked at their eleven-year-old daughter, my thoughts would turn to Marilyn. Although the evening was swell, it made me very homesick. Naturally, you can understand the mixture of moods I went through.

We left, reluctantly, at 9:30 p.m. and the taste of the dinner was the main topic for conversation the balance of the evening. I can only hope for a speedy victory so that all of use can have Seder together next year. Today was a repetition of other days. No new development. Getting most of our equipment ready to bivouac next week. They took our pup tents and waterproofed them.

*April 9, 1944*

My Darling,

We have a night problem each night of this coming week. Then next Sunday, we have to have all of our equipment clean for inspection prior to going on bivouac. It must appear odd to you that I speak so much of bivouac, but the reason for it is that it's the final phase of our training period and has been the subject of conversation since our arrival here. You can understand my impatience in regards to its finality.

Have just gotten the group picture I wrote of and have mailed it to you. On my left in the picture is Dave and on my right is a fellow who is a German refugee. His name is Sigmund Hersch. We are the only Jewish soldiers in the company.

*April 10, 1944*

Went to the show last night and gratefully saw a picture that did not have a war sequence. *You Can't Ration Love* was the name of it. Amusing in spots, at least there was lots of music and it was light. Came back to the barracks afterward and then read a while before falling off to sleep.

Just started to rain again, although it is quite warm. This is truly a blue Monday. Dreary, rain and a sad horse opera coming in over the radio. We are sitting on our bunks. Some of the men are cleaning their rifles, some are writing letters. Others merely dozing off. No one seems to be saying much. You can almost see their trains of thought in their faces. Wives, children, and home are uppermost in their minds. It's getting so close to furlough time that we think of nothing else.

*April 12, 1944*

Things are moving along quite speedily now, the finish of our cycle is not far off now. Most of the problems we go through now are more or less just a review. Our problems at night are just a joke, we do almost nothing except flounder around in the darkness and try and sleep when we are allowed to sit down. It turned very cold in the past few days and the nights are remindful of Balboa in dead winter.

Gosh, honey, there just isn't anymore I can write. I know you wouldn't be interested in the work I did on KP today. I guess I mopped fifteen miles in floors, and probably washed eighteen thousand cups. You can imagine what it's like. Nothing much else dear, except I don't like the idea of you letting everyone feel your inflated bra—you mean the female sex only, don't you?

*April 15, 1944*

Getting all readied up for the bivouac, we start out early Monday morning. Did all of my laundry this afternoon and did a nice job of it. Am certainly surprised to hear about Leona's husband getting shipping orders. There certainly must be something gone haywire.

The latest instruction from commanding headquarters states that men over twenty-six are not to be sent into combat zones. If his condition is as bad as he claims, he can't possibly be shipped over. I would like to tell of at least fifteen men in our company who have gotten medical discharges for ailments that are ridiculous. In order for Bill to be sent over, his record must show seventeen weeks of basic training and must also show that he is physically capable of going into combat. Tell Lee not to worry, in my opinion he will be stationed here.

P.S. Kiss the Duchess. Pardon the penmanship. I am writing this on the ground.

*April 21, 1944*

My Darling,

They are working the hell out of us out here, but I am rather glad for it, for it keeps us from fully realizing just how uncomfortable it really is. This is as close to actual battle conditions we will get without being in the real thing. Sleeping on the cold hard ground, not being able to wash, and snakes, lizards, and all the other things that go with the great outdoors. I am afraid I'll never be a tall, silent, outdoor man. Give me a Simmons bed anytime. I haven't taken my clothes off since Monday. We have to sleep in them and do I stink! Of course, we eat our chow from our mess kits—ants, flies and all. You don't mind that much when you are hungry. There are only seven more days left of this and I'll be a happy man when it's over with.

P.S. Kiss the Duchess. Also received two letters from her today.

*April 23, 1944*

Sunday again, just had mail call and received two letters from you. The box of Yosts came; also, the fruit is delicious. Thank you for it. Have been working very hard and am sure glad this week is over with. They seem to think that this coming week will be much easier. I hope so. It would be wonderful to be able to get into a nice warm shower. I have never been as filthy as I am right now.

Am very tickled about the salami. We will sure do it justice. The food here hasn't been too bad, although there is a good deal of room for improvement. One of the boys said that the mess sergeant was a plumber in civilian life and his cooking makes me believe it. He always forgets to put the important condiments in the food. There is always something missing.

Just about time for chow, dear, so will have to close for now. Wish I knew how to tell you how much I love you.

*May 1, 1944*

My Darling,

The phone call yesterday was the thrill of a lifetime. I can't tell you how much it meant, hearing your's and Marilyn's voices. Never before have I appreciated Mr. Bell's invention.

Received two letters from you and one from the Duchess today. Also, received the sweater. It's a honey. Fits me perfectly and is just the kind I have wanted. Even the fellows commented on it and if the male sex will say nice things about an article of clothing, you must know it's nice.

Just a few more days to go now, my sweet. We expect to sign our furlough papers in the next couple of days.

We had a couple hours of physical training this morning, but we didn't work too hard. There will be more de-processing tomorrow, plus a great deal of physical training. It started to rain Sunday morning and what a rain! It doesn't rain in sheets here; it rains in a full blanket. Right now, the rain is beating down upon the roof of the barracks and we keep wondering if these egg crates will hold up under the terrific pounding.

P.S. Kiss the Duchess. Am going to print my letters now, it's much easier. OK?

*May 3, 1944*

My Darling Chin-up Girl,

Just received your letter containing the pictures and every one of them is swell. Keep looking at them all of the time. The Duchess certainly looks adorable. You seem to have lost weight, did you? Couldn't write to you yesterday, we had to make a long march and didn't get in until midnight.

We are still de-processing, will probably turn our rifles and equipment in Friday. The main topic of conversation centers on our next compound and where we will most likely be shipped. Naturally, no one knows; all of us are guessing and hoping for assignments close to our homes.

Just about time now for chow, so will have to close, kept two pictures and am returning the balance. 'Till tomorrow.

> I love you very much.
> Joe

P.S. Kiss the Duchess for me.

*May 4, 1944*

My Darling,

I can realize just how tired you must be. Fervently wish you didn't have to work, but there's nothing I can do about it now. Still de-processing, as we will be until Saturday. Took all of my equipment and gave it a GI bath, so that everything will be in good shape for the final inspection Saturday. Had it quite easy today, they let us catch up on some badly needed rest. We signed our furlough papers also, which does not mean a thing, as orders can be changed at the last minute.

Dave and myself went to Tyler last night to indulge in a steak. Certainly was delicious. After we went to the show, and saw *Destination Tokyo*.

Rained continually until this afternoon and the sun has just come out for the first time this week. Made good use of the sweater. Am going to have dinner at the service club now, and then sit around a while and watch the kids jitterbug. Then to bed. Have to be up early tomorrow. We have a seven and one-half mile speed march scheduled. It will wind up the cycle for us and it will make me very happy. If I don't hear the word *march* the rest of my life, I'll be very well satisfied.

Nothing much else to write, so am closing for now. Miss you terribly and the days can't pass quickly enough for me. Never believed I could love anyone as deeply as I love you.

'Till tomorrow.

> Yours forever,
> Joe

P.S. Kiss the Duchess. Received the Yosts package from Carrie.

*May 7, 1944*

Know just how you felt taking that ride and the night being romantic. Fell asleep after reading your letter, and dreamt about you. Enjoyed it immensely though and a couple more like that until I get home won't hurt me. Don't be alarmed; it's a normal reaction, and the Army field manual says that if it doesn't happen, then it's time to see a doctor.

*May 9, 1944*

No news yet of my furlough; they seem to take their own sweet time about everything, so I just have to be patient.

Most of the boys who are shipping out have already started turning in their equipment. There will be about forty of us left in the whole company. The ones that are left are mostly young fellows who volunteered for the parachute troops and their transfer orders have not come down from Battalion Headquarters as yet. Of those who weren't in the parachute troops, they are either physically unfit for combat or are waiting for special gas mask glasses.

Dave and myself are quite puzzled and are naturally wondering what they have in store for us.

*May 10, 1944*

Weather has been very hot these last few days. Reminds me of California weather. Turns a bit cool at night. Millions of stars in the Texas sky—takes me back to those beautiful nights in the San Jacinto Mountains, remember? Never before realized how wonderful memories can be. I can remember so clearly how your nose would wrinkle up when you laughed and how your pretty eyes would light up when you were pleased, your graceful walk and soft voice, except when the Duchess wouldn't eat. I keep thinking about all these things and hoping I can enjoy them again.

*May 12, 1944*

There are just twenty of us left now from our company; the rest of them shipped out today. Age makes no difference; all of them have to report to Maryland on the 31st of this month. From there they will probably ship overseas. Yes, honey, I did get a break not being on the shipping list. I don't know why they are holding me and the only ones that do know are Camp Headquarters. They, of course, will not tell you a thing. I'm praying for a real good break. I just have to be patient and perhaps I may get my new assignment next week. Everyone gets a ten-day furlough, plus traveling time, when they leave camp so don't worry, honey, I'll get one too.

We are getting a new crop of rookies for the new cycle. Supposed to be here Sunday. Most of them are from Chicago. Incidentally, we are not rookies anymore; we have graduated and are now known as buck privates.

*May 16, 1944*

Received your letter today it made me very happy to learn you were pleased with the roses. If red roses can express an undying love, I hope they were the reddest ever. Your letter pleased me to no end and I read it and reread it.

No news yet of any furloughs. *Latrino* rumors still persist and as I wrote you the other day, the latest *latrino*-gram has it that we may be shipped by this coming Thursday.

There were seventy-nine fellows in on the train this morning; they came from Greenland, where they have been stationed for thirty-two months. They are here to become instructors. The stories they tell aren't very encouraging. I hope yours and my prayers won't go unanswered: it would make me very happy to stay in the USA.

P.S. Kiss the Duchess. Have you received the pin I sent to her? Where did Leona's husband wind up? Regards to everyone—am going to sleep now hoping for one of those dreams of you.

# 5

# The Furlough

The Army furloughed Joe from May 19 through the first week in June. Marilyn recalled a few things about his visit, such as meeting him at the bus stop when he first arrived home. Much of their time was spent in Balboa and Los Angeles. Ten days later Joe shipped out again, this time to Camp Rucker in Alabama. My mother vividly remembered being at Union Station and seeing her father in formation with other soldiers. She remembered him picking her up and carrying her as they walked. She remembered watching him kiss her mother good-bye. And that this was the last time she ever saw him.

Joe and family at Balboa Beach

Gertie, ready
to roll

Joe in the
Fun Zone at
Balboa Beach

Gertie, posing

# 6

# Into the Fire, So to Speak

*June 7, 1944*

Am finally able to write you. Arrived in Ozark Sunday evening and since my arrival, things have been in quite turmoil. I fell from the frying pan into the fire, so to speak.

Reported into camp Monday noon and was put into the casual detachment until yesterday. Am now a rifleman in CoA of the 262nd Infantry. I was willing to do anything except become a rifleman. The administrative and training on my orders were just so much hooey, as was the high IQ. Neither meant anything! The basic training I just finished is to be continued here and if I have ever needed your moral support, I need it now. Since my induction into the Army, my spirits have never been so low. Thought perhaps I could get some kind of break such as being in the headquarters company or in an office of some kind, but no, they not only put me in the toughest branch of the service but also in the toughest company. As yet, I haven't been assigned to any platoon and I am going to try and keep from being put into one.

My trip out here was the worst ever. To begin with, saying good-bye to you and the Duchess was the hardest thing I have ever done. There was so much I wanted to say to you and didn't know how. I wanted to tell you how wonderful the ten days were and that they were the happiest ten days of my life. Wanted to tell you, too, how wonderful you were and how much I love you. The quick good-bye was best though and I know you understand how I felt.

You can imagine how badly I felt on the train. Didn't get any sleep until Sunday night. Trains were overcrowded and unbearably hot. Each change of trains was made in the space of one-half hour, so I was only able to send you the one post card. As far as Alabama is concerned, all I need to say is "Tobacco Road." I think that can pretty well describe the state. Everything and everybody needs a coat of paint.

Sweet, I can't put my feelings into words. I am so very homesick and am thoroughly disgusted. It's very hard to come into a new camp not knowing a soul. Have to make new friends and it's going to be very hard. The fellows here all seem so unfriendly. I hope it's just my imagination. Most of the fellows are youngsters and have been in the Army at least ten months or more. They all seem to be from New York and New Jersey. At least I don't have to listen to any southern drawls.

Well, my sweet, today is the Duchess's birthday and my thoughts go back to Friday night nine years ago at about 6 p.m. Seems like yesterday and hard to believe our baby is such a big girl. May God grant me the privilege of being with both of you on her next birthday.

P.S. Kiss the Duchess and tell her many happy returns. Have you heard from Dave? I hope he doesn't get the tough break I did.

*June 8, 1944*

I can't tell you how anxious I am to hear from you. My letter yesterday must have sounded quite dishearten-ing, but I know you will understand how badly I felt. I am so disgusted that I don't want to write you of the things I am doing. They put me into the first platoon and we are doing the same things I have done for seventeen weeks. I can't take this slow torture, honey, and rather than make this a long drawn out affair, I'd rather go overseas and get it over with fast. Oh honey, I feel so miserable and downhearted. It's awful my writing you of these things, but somehow I can't help it. You have always been so understanding and comforting that I thought writing you of my despon-dency might ease my mind a bit.

*June 10, 1944*

My Darling,

Once again, I partake of the generosity of the USO and here I am writing to you from their club in Ozark, Alabama. Had nothing to do this afternoon, so I thought I'd come to town, have dinner, and take in a show.

No mail from you as yet, looking forward to your letters is the most important thing in my life right now. Waiting through the mail call and not getting your letter gives me a very empty feeling. I am hoping for a letter from you tomorrow.

More drill this morning, in an intensive heat. What do they expect to accomplish with all of this additional training, I don't know. As I wrote you in a previous letter, we are going through the same things I had in my basic training. I have never hated anything as much in all of my life.

I told you of my going to chapel last night. I went for the Friday evening services.

Unfortunately, I did not meet anyone, for immediately following the services, everyone left. I am going again tomorrow and perhaps I may be able to find someone to talk to.

Nothing more to write, sweet, so am closing for now. Honey, I love you and miss you terribly.

Joe

P.S. My regards to everyone. No letters to them until I am in a better frame of mind. Kiss the duchess for me. How is she getting on?

*June 12, 1944*

My Darling,

Got up rather late yesterday and had breakfast at the service club. At 11:00 a.m., I went to services at the chapel. From there, we were all invited to the temple in Dothan. It's about an hour's ride from here and is much bigger than Ozark. At least there is a great deal more life in Dothan. Arriving at the temple we were served a brunch consisting of pickled herring, potato salad, rye bread, cookies, and iced coffee. The rabbi then made a speech and we were entertained by an amateur magician. I enjoyed the black magic. I left the temple about three in the afternoon and strolled around the town. Went to the show, saw *Hey, Rookie.* Came back to camp about 8 p.m. and got caught in a terrific rainstorm. Was soaking wet by the time I got to the barracks, so took my clothes off and fell asleep.

The weather has been extremely hot. We are wet from the time we get up until we go to bed. Believe me the guy who wrote *Dear Old Southland* didn't mean Alabama.

*June 14, 1944*

Your second letter made me realize how wrong I was in taking this Army life the way I have been for the past two weeks. You are the most wonderful chin-up girl in the world and it is I who is proud of you. I am always amazed at the effect your letters have upon me. They seem to give me a shot in the arm.

So the Duchess enjoyed her birthday. It's so hard to believe she is nine. Won't be very long and she will be going on dates. It has always been my ambition to be her first date, dear; afterwards, she can have as many as she likes. How is she getting along with the piano? Does she practice as much as ever?

Truly, honey, I feel much better now and it is all because of your letters. All I want to explain is the fact that my mood wasn't brought on by the reason of my being in the infantry, it was due to the knowledge that I had to go through the exact training procedure that I had already had at Fannin. Again, the disgust I had can be blamed upon the manner in which the Army builds up your hopes and then tears them down without the remotest explanation. You know how hopeful I was of being put into some sort of administrative work and my orders implied that very thing, and then come down here and have to do the things I thought were all over with, it sort of broke down what little morale I had left. If it weren't for your very wonderful letters, honey, I know I couldn't possibly take it.

The news from La La in Detroit was quite a shock. Marty Cohen's untimely passing, and Pitt overseas. Hard to believe that of Pitt. I had the impression that he could con his way out of going over. But I suppose that is one thing you can't buy your way out of.

The stories around here still persist that pre-Pearl Harbor fathers are going to stay on this side for quite some time. I heard the same thing at Fannin. But you know the Army, anything can happen. I only hope it is true. We had quite a few new men in today who were at Fort Meade ready to go across; for some reason they were sent here instead. Most of them are from Fannin. I don't know any of them as they were in the 56th Regiment. It would be swell if Dave were sent here too, from Meade.

*June 18, 1944*

My Darling,

Received the two Father's Day cards and I loved them. The sentiments in each were swell. I wrote that I would probably go to chapel this morning, but I didn't know I was to be on KP today. Consequently, I had to miss the brunch and also had to delay writing to the folks.

Just found out that starting tomorrow, we are to have a six weeks basic training course and our hours are to be from 6 a.m. until 10 p.m. After the six-week period, we are to go on maneuvers. It will be a miracle if I make it. Something wonderful to look forward to, isn't it?

I sent Justin a letter last night. Let me know if he received it. How is he getting along? And his mother-in-law, is she getting any better? It must be a terrible thing to see how brokenhearted she is. I keep thinking about the tragedy, knowing nothing can be done about it. Do you know just what happened? I can't figure it out.

Gosh, honey, it's so hard to think of anything to write. Nothing of any interest ever happens here. I have made a few acquaintances, but somehow I prefer to keep to myself. I can't explain it. All I do is think of you and Duchess and those thoughts keep me going. I have your picture on my shelf and my bed is situated so that I face it. I always talk to you each night before *lights-out* and somehow I feel that you can sense it. I hope you do.

P.S. Thank the Duchess for her wonderful card. Please kiss her for me and tell her I love her.

*June 19, 1944*

My Darling,

Received two letters and a swell box of See's candy today. The letter, candy, and the pictures were perfect. Got a big kick out of the pictures, you don't spoil them in any way. I am the one that spoils them.

Things are just the same as ever. You write that Bill hopes I didn't get the same kind of break as the Fannin boys at his camp. You can tell him I am doing the same thing as they are doing. The heat is still up to par and there is no relief in sight. If it were only cooler, I know I could take this a lot better. Haven't heard from Detroit as yet, but you know how the boys are; when they get ready to write, they will.

Am happy that Justin is feeling a bit better and I hope Mrs. Rosen is getting to the point where she will recover. From what you tell me, the Duchess is getting along wonderfully. It makes me very happy and proud. Not that I haven't always been proud of her, just that I never realized how wonderful she really is until that ten-day furlough.

P.S. Kiss the Duchess. Regards to everyone. Has Dave left for Meade yet?

*June 22, 1944*

There isn't any news of any kind. We have been going through the same procedure every day. We are now learning how to shoot the rifle. That is laughable. I have done nothing else for the past six months and now they want to teach it to us all over again. The biggest laugh of them all is the fact that they are teaching the fellows who just came back from overseas the same thing. There is a staff sergeant in our platoon who was in the invasion of Sicily and received a citation for killing seven Germans in the initial landing, and he, too has to learn to fire the rifle. The Army sure does funny things.

Hasn't been any change in the training and rumors are flying thick and fast. The latest is that we will move out of here by August 10. I don't believe anything I hear until I see it. They have shipped quite a few of the fellows from here to Fort Meade.

Out in the field all morning and noticed a funny thing. You remember my telling you of the millions of roses around the training areas of Fannin? There are no roses here, but there are tons of blackberries. You know how I love them so. I had quite a time. They grow wild and are the big luscious variety.

*June 23, 1944*

We took a nine-mile march this morning; the temperature was not less than one hundred degrees at any time during the march. A complete battalion started it and about half of them came in under their own power. The other half passed out alongside the road. Thought that I was going to make it, but I reached about three-quarters of the trek and couldn't go any more. Dropped out just before I was ready to pass out. A couple of other men and myself made it to a stream and upon reaching it, we dove in headfirst— clothes, rifles, and packs! Never knew how wonderful water really is until today. Certainly was quite an experience. Haven't heard from anyone except you and the Duchess, no fan mail or anything. How is our wonderful baby getting along? Gosh, I miss the both of you.

*June 24, 1944*

Have been reading most of the day and trying my best to keep cool. You'd think we were in the tropics, the manner in which we lie around in our barracks. We are all lying around, reading and writing letters, most of us stark naked and no one saying anything. Their thoughts, I imagine, are like mine—thinking of home and how we would be spending this kind of Sunday if we were at home. How wonderful the word *home* sounds.

*June 29, 1944*

My Darling,
    Received the package today and everything was perfect. Tickled pink with the soap, too.
    Was out of everything that you sent me. We are still training and it sure does get tougher each day. The extreme heat makes it twice as bad. Hope Abe finds a place at Balboa. It would be swell for you and the Duchess to spend the holiday there. Wish I could go with you.
    Sorry to hear about Bill passing out in the retreat parade. I know what it's like and I have seen healthier men than him do the same thing. Surprised that Leona is going back to New York, but I imagine she will feel that she is much closer to Bill.
    Tomorrow night is chapel and two Jewish fellows and myself are going. They are both from New York and were shipped to Fort Meade after their basic. They were held there a week and then sent down here. One's name is Al Benson, and the other is Lou Rubenstein.

After chow tonight, I looked through my pockets and found I had twenty-one cents, so I bought myself a candy bar and went to the show with the fifteen cents I had left. Now here I am, almost penniless except for the copper penny I have left. It brings me back to the time when you and I got up one morning at the Detroiter and found ourselves in that situation. You took it all in stride and never complained. I am marveling at the wonderful way in which you combated trouble, how cool you have always been. I have never done anything to deserve having someone like you love me and I am extremely lucky and proud to be able to say you are my wife. Honey, when this is all over, we are going to be so happy. I've had so much time to think and plan and I have so much confidence in the future.

*June 30, 1944*

Your short note with the ten dollars enclosed got here today and again it came just in time. It really was a lifesaver and I'll return it as soon as I am paid. Also received a very cute letter from Jackie. I laughed all day thinking of one paragraph in his letter. He mentioned that fact, "while I am writing this letter, mother and Aunt Gert are sitting on the patio, smoking and talking. I don't know what they are saying because they are talking to each other in very low voices." I can't begin to tell you how I laughed when I read that. From now on, the two of you will have to talk in a normal tone of voice, else how can my reporter give me a report on your activities and conversations?

We had a retreat parade today all of us dressed in Class A uniforms and looking very regimental. The sun boiled all the starch in our uniforms and honestly if I had urinated in my pants, I couldn't have noticed the difference; that's how wet we were after getting back to our barracks.

Just came into the USO from Dothan Temple, where Lou, Al, and myself had brunch. We witnessed a wedding ceremony in the temple, performed for a soldier and his girlfriend. Took me back almost eleven years ago. Seems like yesterday that you and I stood under the canopy and kissed each other after the rabbi's blessing. Lou played the Hammond organ for the couple and we injected a bit of humor after the ceremony.

*July 1, 1944*

My Darling,

Funny that business at the store is low ebb; one would think you would be quite busy before a holiday.

Had KP again today and got through about 5:30 p.m. I didn't work too hard. As a matter of fact, I snuck out during the afternoon and did most of my laundry; now I won't have to worry about it tomorrow. Lou and Al, the two boys I wrote you about, went swimming and since they hadn't gotten back by the time I was ready to leave, I came to town alone. We are going to Dothan and I know the three of us will enjoy some Jewish food. Am going to the one and only theater here after I finish this letter. Will buy myself a box of popcorn and sit through a western with Roy Rogers as the star. Some fun, eh?

*July 4, 1944*

Independence Day again, a national holiday for everyone except the soldier at Camp Rucker. It was the same as any other day, except perhaps, we worked a bit harder.

Every once in a while, the mess sergeant comes up with a fairly good dinner, we call it *supper* in the Army, and tonight was one of those times. Potato salad made just right, cold cuts, iced tea, and one-fourth of the most delicious watermelon I have ever had. I believe that is the only redeeming feature of the South. Their watermelons are superb. The first time I have honestly enjoyed my dinner in the mess hall.

We made that twelve-mile hike this morning and I did just get in. Couldn't move for an hour after getting back to the barracks. Then to top it off, this afternoon we were out in the field digging various kinds of foxholes. I'll be an expert ditch digger after the war. I can just see myself tossing a shovelful of dirt out of a ditch and you coming down the road, bringing me my lunch pail.

*July 6, 1944*

Out on a problem most of the day. We dug more foxholes; after digging them, we had to fill them up again and then march three miles back to the barracks in a driving rain. Has been raining quite steadily and we certainly appreciate it

They had a revue at the camp theatre called *This Is the 66th*. Just ended and I came here to the service club to write you. The show was made up of camp talent and if I couldn't produce a show any better than the one I just saw, it was pitiful! Just like a high school show. As a matter of fact, I have seen high school shows that were great compared to this one.

### *July 7, 1944*

They put me on this hospital guard and it was my duty to sit in front of the prison ward and allow no one in or out without proper authority. The balance of the wards in my post were the rehabilitation wards and it is the most pitiful sight, seeing these young boys walking to and fro with an appearance of total disregard for anyone or anything. Shattered nerves and shattered minds. War is truly hell. An interesting if sorrowful sidelight was a young fellow, who appeared to be about twenty-four, taking his morning walk. He had to pass in front of me and before he went by me, I noticed that his right hand shook as though he had St. Vitus' Dance. I had a loaded carbine slung on my shoulder and upon confronting me, he stopped, became highly agitated, and burst into tears. The sight of the rifle unnerved him and I found from his orderly that the fellow was gun-shy due to the fact that he had shot someone while on guard duty. His mind cracked and now they are trying to rehabilitate him.

### *July 8, 1944*

Drill and more drill, getting so that I hear those drill commands in my sleep. Sat in recreation room and watched the youngsters jitterbug a while. Amazing, the difficult contortions and positions they get themselves in. Got quite a kick out of it.

No mail from my brothers, although I have been writing to them quite regularly. They must be quite busy with the park and picking horses at the track, so I kind of think that when they get a free moment, they will write.

Felt so good, reading of the fun you and the Duchess had over the holiday. She loves you so much honey and I don't blame her. I do too. What is it that you have got, that Grable hasn't got?

*July 9, 1944*

My Darling,

Haven't received any mail from anyone but you; an occasional letter from the Showmen's reaches me. Sure would like to hear from the boys. What is Babe going to do? Am anxious to know just what his plans are. How are the Schneiders? Does Abe go to Balboa every night?

Joe

P.S. Kiss the Duchess. Got a thrill out of your wish to the moon. I too make a wish every night. Keep thinking of those wonderful nights we had on my furlough.

*July 11, 1944*

My Darling,

Two letters from you—was so glad the missing letter turned up; I have been worried about it. I can well understand what a mad house Sak's must be and it isn't any wonder that you are all knocked out at the end of the day. It sounded as though most of the customers were people you knew.

They made me barracks orderly today, which meant that I didn't have to go out on the field and drill. It was my duty to clean the barracks and also the latrine, and then see that the building was kept clean all day. It's the one job all of us would like to get permanently. Lots of time to sleep in the afternoon and I sure took advantage of it.

Tomorrow is the 12th, and payday for those of use who haven't already been paid. I haven't even the one cent that I wound up with a couple of weeks ago, so tomorrow's pay will be appreciated no end. I'll enclose the ten dollars in my letter to you.

Am writing to you from the camp library, have been doing quite a bit of reading lately. It seems to ease my mind. Have read a few good medical books and read quite a few interesting articles. There was something that always puzzled me about the Duchess and in reading, I found the answer. You know how carsick she gets when she goes for a ride of any distance? I always had the idea that it was the motion of the car that caused it, but I found that her stomach ache, as she calls it, is brought about by the carbon monoxide fumes from the motor. Carbon monoxide is a poison gas that is tasteless, colorless, and invisible, and children are very susceptible to it. The doctor that wrote about it gave Marilyn's symptoms to a T. He said that regardless of how cold the weather is, always keep a window open in the car, especially if there are children in it and never allow a child to lie on the floor of a car. I can easily understand why she gets so nauseous.

I believe I had better stop now or I'll probably go into a long lecture on various ailments of the body.
I'm so in love with you.
Joe

P.S. Don't forget the Duchess. Regards to everyone.

*July 12, 1944*

My Darling,

Your letter today was swell, makes me so proud that the Duchess is so grown up.

Immediately after mail call this noon, my first sergeant informed me that I would have to turn in all of my equipment, as I was being sent to Fort Meade in the morning. Quite a shocking surprise, but that's the way they do things in the Army. I have no idea as to where they will send me from there. Hope I can get some kind of break for a change. The fact that I'm going to Meade does not mean that I am to be sent overseas; from there they can send me any place in the US.

I am hoping against hope that I can be stationed near home. Of course, that's one of those miracles, but it has happened to other fellows and it can happen to me.

*July 13, 1944*

As I said in yesterday's letter, going to Meade does not mean that I am going overseas; as matter of act, I am firmly convinced that I won't. They are not sending men over that are pre-Pearl Harbor fathers or men that have reached the age of thirty-two. So you see, I

have two good things going for me and all I need is
a little luck.

*July 14, 1944*

Just took my barracks bag up to the truck so they
could put it on the train. The four of us from our
company are leaving here at 2 p.m. We figure to arrive
at Meade Saturday morning, so in the event that you
don't hear from me for a few days, it will be because
of the fact that I won't know for a least twenty-four
hours after getting to Meade what my APO number
is.

Received your letter yesterday and you know how
much I enjoyed it. Got paid this morning, so am
enclosing ten dollars I owe you. You finally got the
bond from the Army.

Have had it very easy for the past few days. The
hardest work I've done is to try and dodge the first
sergeant so that he couldn't put me on any detail.
Slept in the woods all afternoon and yesterday night,
next to a rippling stream under a big shady pecan
tree. If it weren't for the chigger bites, it would have
been perfect.

# 7

# A Million
# Blinking Stars

There are one hundred fifteen of us from Camp
Rucker and I have no idea as to what they are going to
do with us. This is by far the largest camp I have been
in so far. It's immense and it isn't like an Army base at
all. The civilians come in and out without question.
Most of the men here have their wives with them and
it's an odd sight to see so many women around an
Army camp. It's so different from that Alabama heat.
At least we can breathe here.

Am hoping and praying for a good break.

*July 18, 1944*

Well, honey, this looks like the real thing now. They
tell us we are going overseas. Of course, I still have the

idea that I will be kept on this side. From here, we will be sent to a POE and at that point, I am convinced I will be sent to a camp in the States. This is a POR, or Port of Replacement, and the Port of Embarkation has the final word on our disposition. They have sent thousands of men back from the POE, so I haven't given up hope.

I went to Baltimore last night and it was like a shot in the arm. It's a real city and everything seemed so natural. Bright lights and the hustle and bustle of a real live town. So different from the monotony of the sleepy, unawakened, unwashed hamlets of the South. Had a few drinks over a bar and then had some wonderful Chinese food, for which I have had a yen on for quite some time. Strolled through the downtown section during the course of the evening and stopped in front of a nightclub called the "21 Club." Lo and behold, they were featuring Jerry and Turk; you remember the team that was such a hit at Dave Saks! Went in, had a couple of drinks, and caught the show. Talked to the Turk for quite a while after the show. He didn't know me until I mentioned the Detroiter, and then he not only remembered me, but also asked about my wife and daughter. He remembers having seen us around the hotel.

Had some real laughs for the first time in so long.

*July 20, 1944*

That telephone call last night was the hype that I needed. Just hearing your voice did so much toward buoyancy of my spirits. I realize the news I had for you was the worst ever, but I felt that if I received orders to go across, you would want to know. My shipping orders were as great a shock to me as anything I can remember. It is still hard to believe, I have been so confident that I was to be kept here. Well, honey, I am only one of ten million and I know I have to go. Don't worry about me, 'cause I won't be anywhere near a combat zone. They will probably assign me to an occupational force and I will be quite far from any combat.

This letter will probably be the last one that won't be censored and there will be times that I may want to tell you things that are censored, so in my letters from wherever I may be, look for an unusual sentence or word. I can't use code or any language but English, so I'll try and tell you where I am by asking questions about different people or places. We don't know where we are going until we get to the POE. If we don't ship out from there right away and if we are near New York, I'll try to get a pass to New York and call you.

There isn't much else I can write, honey, so I'll close now knowing you've got your chin up and are confident that I'll be home soon with the two people I love most. Things always work out for the best and with your wonderful love and faith, I know I'll be safe and will be with you soon.

P.S. Don't tell the Duchess, honey. Kiss her for me. I'll dream of you every night. Regards to all.

*July 21, 1944*

I've got the funniest kind of feeling in the pit of my stomach. I suppose it's due to the fact that I am scared to death. I'll get over it, I know, but just the same, it sure is an uncomfortable feeling.

P.S. A big kiss for the Duchess. I wrote you yesterday about my using odd names and places to tell you things that I want you to know. I will use full names, as we are not allowed to use nicknames or just the first or last names. Also, be sure to look for any sentences that apparently have no meaning or are of any importance. Gosh, I miss you so much.

*July 22, 1944*

Darling Chin-up Girl,

Censorship of all my letters will make it quite difficult to write a newsy letter, but I will do the best that I am allowed.

Am still in the good old USA, at a point along the eastern seaboard. No doubt, I will be on the *banana boat* in the near future.

The night we left Meade, there were a million blinking stars in the sky and I kept looking up at them. Somehow, I felt that you were looking at them too, and I thought that perhaps you whispered a prayer or two. I did and all I asked for was a successful completion of our mission so I could come back home to you and the Duchess. I'll be back, honey; don't you worry.

There isn't much more I can write, dear, so I'll close for now. I am so pleased that the Duchess is doing so well in school. Kiss her for me and please don't say anything to her about my being transferred. Just tell her I am still in Fort Meade.

*July 23, 1944*

Have been sitting here in the service club for quite some time, wondering what to write you. This being limited to written thoughts and phrases does not appeal to me. After having poured out my heart to you for so many weeks, and now to be forcibly weaned away from the attempt to write you of Army life as seen through my eyes, is quite disconcerting and not at all to my liking.

Your letters, if you have written any since my leaving Meade, have not reached me as yet. Their conspicuous absence is the darkest of all the dark spots in my present mode of living. I look for your letter hungrily, knowing I must have patience.

I am not allowed to venture even a guess as to my future nor am I allowed to say anything of current events. The only course left open is the past. I keep remembering all the pleasant things we used to do. Each day that passes, I look back a year ago and try to remember what we were doing at that particular time. Last year June 24, remember how busy we were preparing for our trip to Detroit? We were so worried about the tires and as always, you were right; they should have been re-treaded. But with all the bad breaks, we did have fun. What a perfect lady Marilyn was and how she acted the part of a well-seasoned traveler. Perhaps those wonderful days will return. I have so much faith in the future.

P.S. Regards to everyone. Reminding you again that your letters to me are not censored, so you can write things that are of a personal nature. A thought just occurred to me; I wonder who censors the censor's mail? Rather a pertinent question. I miss you and the Duchess so very much.

# 8

# Overseas

This is truly the first opportunity I have had to write you. We have been kept quite busy and it seemed as though there aren't enough hours in the day.

"Somewhere in England," that is as much as I can tell you in reference to my present location. It's hard to believe that I am actually using the phrase "somewhere in England." You know that I wasn't at all convinced that I would go overseas and to be here now seems unreal.

There isn't much I am allowed to tell you of our crossing, except that it was safe and quite smooth. I became a bit seasick at one time but got over it quickly.

The balance of your mail caught up with me before I left and I enjoyed each letter immensely. Have been thinking of you and the Duchess constantly each night. I try to imagine what the both of you are doing. Miss both of you terribly.

*August 8, 1944*

Received three letters from you and one from the Duchess in which she enclosed some of her knitting. I was thrilled beyond words; it seems to be a knitted doll's dress, and I can assure you I will carry it with me no matter where I go. Your letters sounded swell, I knew you would shake off that depressive feeling.

Yours truly,
Joey

P.S. Regards to everyone. Gosh! A year ago today, we were on our way to Tijuana, Mexico, remember? What a time we had!

*August 12, 1944*

Sitting here in a foxhole somewhere in France, it's difficult to believe that I am so far away from you and the Duchess. My thoughts of both of you shorten that distance and each memory brings me closer to home.

I feel fine, honey, and I don't want you to worry about me. I have a comfortable foxhole and sleep well.

I didn't stay in England long enough to really give you a good word picture of it. The things I did see were quite interesting. Gray stone houses all alike, miles and miles of farmland, the conspicuous absence of outdoor advertising, and the manner in which the English utilize every bit of space. Here too, in France, the farmhouses and city dwellings are of gray stone. On our ride to our present destination, we passed numerous French villages and if you think back to the Long Beach earthquake in 1938, you can almost visualize how these villages look. Practically nothing left of them. The buildings that are standing have large gaping holes in them. It is amazing how accurate our Air Force and artillery are. Even as I sit here, *[censored—about one sentence of the letter was apparently cut out by army censors]* roar overhead flying their ways to their respective missions. I know each bomb, each shell, and each bullet is another nail in Hitler's coffin. The French people themselves are a tired and battered people. It is a constant wonder how they have stood this tragedy of war. Yet here they are coming back to their villages and homes, or rather what is left of the buildings and villages, ready to try and pick up where they left off. I hope, as millions of us are hoping, that it is over soon and all of us can live in peace and happiness.

Yours always,
Joey

P.S. Don't use V-mail. It's too slow. Am enclosing some French money, the kind we get paid. Just souvenirs—they are worth twenty cents apiece. Give one to Jackie and the Duchess.

*August 14, 1944*

Been feeling fine and I believe the weather has a great deal to do with it. Swell, sunshiny days thus far, only hope it continues.

Just got back from a USO camp show; talent was surprisingly good. No one that we know; the MC hailed from Chicago and two female singers, one a hoofer and the other a canary. Both of them lookers and sold their stuff well. Comic juggler got a big hand. The MC did a Bergen set and he too had to beg off. All of them worked hard, and believe me, these traveling shows deserve a lot of credit for the work they are doing. It's very difficult to sell yourself to an audience with the roar of guns as a background.

Not much I can tell you at this time, except that I have a comfortable foxhole—no running hot and cold water of course, but it is the best I can get under the circumstances. Am closing now, loving you and the Duchess deeply. Anxiously awaiting your letters.

*August 17, 1944*

To date, I haven't received any mail, though I am expecting it daily. Feel fine and this outdoor life isn't too bad. Of course, I miss those wonderful warm showers and that swell soft bed. Sleeping in a bed seems to be something I did in the distant dim past.

The weather here is about the same as it is in the States, a typical warm August month. Grass is green, flowers in bloom, apple trees bending to the weight of their seasonal crop. Each farm has an apple orchard and cider is plentiful, the hard variety. The French concoct a drink called *calvados*, somewhere in the neighborhood of two hundred eighty proof. It's a cross between a boilermaker and two tons of TNT. I use it in my lighter as lighter fluid. Works fine.

Red Cross club mobile visited the neighborhood today, treated the boys to coffee and doughnuts and canned music. Surprising how big an event it is to us. Reminds me of the thrill I used to get when the circus paid its yearly visit to town.

Well, my sweet, nothing much else I can write; you know that you and the Duchess are in my thoughts constantly. I hope she has been writing to me. No doubt, your letters, when I receive them, will tell me all the news I hunger for.

*August 18, 1944*

Wish your mail would catch up with me, seems as though I haven't heard from you in years.

We were entertained by no less than Dinah Shore today, through the courtesy of the USO. Worked wonderfully well and as always, she had to beg off. Sang to audience requests, her rich, full voice and her rendition of numbers caused many a twinge of home-sickness. Her voicing *Paper Doll* took me back to the Detroiter and you, the Duchess, Ruby, and myself, learning the words, remember? *I'll Get By* and the comic number *I Said Yes* were done in typical Shore manner. A talented magician and MC completed the show.

My present location is still a foxhole somewhere in France, more than that I cannot tell you. I feel fine and am not in any danger whatsoever. I try to write you each day, but there are days when it is quite impossible so don't worry about me, it's just that I am quite busy.

*August 20, 1944*

Sunday morning here in France, you are probably just getting ready for bed. I'm trying to picture it. You and the Duchess have just finished listening to the *Hit Parade* and now you are telling her it's time for bed. Naturally, she thinks it's too early and points out that Jackie is still up, but you finally win out and she reluctantly prepares herself for a night's slumber. Am I right?

We have had a bit of rain yet today; the sun keeps ducking behind a cloud-flecked sky. I am sitting here beside a small stream, in which we do all our washing and bathing; everything seems so calm and peaceful. One wouldn't know there was a war going on. Our uniforms and arms bring back the grim reality of bloody conflict. Well, perhaps the time isn't very far away when the Duchess, you, and I can sit beside a stream and bathe in the serenity of a peaceful and happy life.

Not much more that is of any interest so am closing for now. Can only reassure both you and the Duchess of my complete devotion.

*August 24, 1944*

This is the first opportunity I have had to write in the past two days. Just want to let you both know I am fine. Haven't gotten any of your letters as yet, but am hoping they catch up with me soon. May not get a chance to write you for quite some time; but don't worry about me, I'll be OK.

Keep thinking of both of you all the time. Just have faith and it won't be very long and all of us will be together once again. Tell the Duchess to stay with her piano; it's her destiny to make people happy, and she will one day become very famous in the entertainment field. She has show talent, honey; bring it out.

Nothing more. I love you both with all my heart.

Yours lovingly,
Dad

P.S. My best to all the family. Regards to Justin and Al Lewis.

# 9

# The Song Is Over

After August 24, Joe's voice fell silent. The steady cadence in the music of Gertie's life—daily reports from her darling Joey—came abruptly to an end. He would no longer describe his boring days. Or talk about how tired he was. Or complain about the Army. Or ask about mail. Or promise to write. He would no longer ask for money or ask her to send soap, stamps, razors, candy, cigarettes, fudge, strudel, or pictures. He would no longer talk about the latest movies he'd seen, or mention that Dinah Shore sang for his camp. He would never say he hit the jackpot again, that he'd received two letters from her and one from Marilyn on any particular day. No more complaining about the food.

And he would no longer wonder if Slowpoke was keeping up with her piano, and he would never ask Gertie to kiss the Duchess for him again.

On August 29, 1944, Private Joey Moss was killed in action. The liberation of Paris had come a few days prior. After that, the letters Joe hungered for those last few days in France were returned to Gertie and Marilyn with the word *deceased* written in light pencil. Among them was this letter dated August 27, 1944.

*Hello My Dearest Darling,*

*I can see her grow right before my very eyes. When we came home yesterday morning, I told her you were in France, and gave her the francs you sent. Her eyes were as big as saucers and she was thrilled. Then her little face dropped and asked if you were where the bombs were. I told her you assured us that you were safe and not to worry, but that didn't seem to satisfy her. She asked a dozen times since if I was sure you weren't where the bombing is. I wish I was sure. I've been thinking of you constantly, wondering and wondering where you are at each moment of the day. Darling, just think of me at your side because truly, that's where I am most of the time. Flo has caught me thinking out loud so many times. Always the same words:*

*"I wonder where my darling is now."*

*I keep searching the pictures in the newspaper, hoping I might see you in one of them. The papers are full of scenes of the battle of Paris. I keep thinking you were there on that big day. I don't know why. Just a hunch, I guess. I love you my darling always and always. May God watch over you for us, please?*

*Always yours,*
*G.*

# 10

# A Million Twinkling Stars

Months, maybe years after the telegram arrived from Western Union and the letters marked "deceased" were returned, the Army sent Gertrude a handful of my grandfather's personal effects, including a couple of folded-up letters that one can suppose were on his body at the time of death. The letters—one from Gertie, the other from the Duchess—were apparently the last ones he received. They are lightly spotted with what appears to be blood.

From Gertie's letter:

*July 28, 1944*

*The stars were out as bright as ever tonight. I wondered from where you are if you saw them and if your prayers were the same as mine at that particular moment. They twinkled down at me as if to say, "Don't worry, we will watch over him and keep him safe for you." It sort of gave me confidence and for the first time in weeks, my mind felt at ease. I've missed you so terribly, just for the want of your arms around me, even for a few minutes, would have helped. Darling, when you come home, you're sure to have a heck of a time leaving my sight for a minute. Don't think me silly, dear. I love you so much.*

From the Duchess's letter:

*July 16, 1944*

*Tonight we are at Aunt Carrie's house, where I am writing you this letter. I am knitting things again. I wonder if you still have the things I sent you. I am sending you some more things.*
*Good night.*
*Love,*
*Duchess*

Among his other items and personal effects were several smoking pipes, a pipe pouch, a wallet, a Swiss army knife, his lighter, and a small blue and white knitted doll's dress.

# Epilogue

As late as January 1946, a letter to Gertie from Joe's brother Moe indicated that she still mourned the loss of her darling.

> *Gertie,*
>
> *I reread your letter a few times and I want to say this, I know how you feel. Believe me, I do. And honey, I wish you would take a little advice from me. Because I know what lonesomeness is. I've been like that for a long, long time, particularly now that I am getting much older. And I want to tell you honey, you're still a young woman, very good looking. You have everything that you want to live for and enjoy. Go out, and if you meet some nice fellow, don't hesitate. You have a lot of common sense to know who's all right and who isn't. After all, you do want to be happy. And I know darling Joey would want it that way. I know how you feel toward Joey. But after all, honey, you must face facts. And while you're still young. Don't miss an opportunity, because it might be too late someday.*

Although Gertie did date over the years and came close to remarrying, she never did and grew old alone. She passed away in 1980. My mother, the Duchess, after a long battle with cancer, joined them on December 15, 2001. They were reunited as family again.

Joe was temporarily interred in France; but at Gertie's request, he was laid to rest at a veteran's cemetery in San Bruno, California on Thursday, July 2, 1948. My mother always pointed out that the pictures of his burial showed only barren fields. Go there now and all you will see are rows and rows, miles and miles of white headstones.

According to Teri Cram, Joe's niece, Eddie always wanted Joey to go to law school. But Joey dropped out of his pre-legal studies early on, married, sired a daughter, and struggled right up until his death to answer for his shortcomings as a breadwinner. When Joey had to ask Eddie for money, it made both of them uncomfortable. Of course, Eddie wanted to see Joey succeed. But when Joey chose to wear a uniform, maybe Eddie couldn't completely come to terms with the fact that his little brother, a little brother he treated like a son, was in the Army.

That is why the words of Bob Dylan's "Joey" come to mind as the story draws to a close. If Joe Moss's life were a movie, this is the song I would have play over the closing credits. It's not a perfect match, but the symmetries are interesting. The figure in the song, Joey Gallo, was almost the youngest of brothers who "lived off gambling and running numbers, too." I see Eddie as the father figure he became to Joey.

> *Then I saw the old man's limousine head back towards the grave.*
> *I guess he had to say one last goodbye to the son that he could not save.*

*Joey, Joey*
*King of the streets, child of clay—*
*Joey, Joey*
*What made them want to come and blow you away?*

This is the end of our story. Uncertain as to how I could tie it all together—wrap it up, so to speak, and give Joey's story the kind of ending it deserves—I'd like to think I found a suitable coda in an anecdote my grandmother told about my grandfather.

After he reported for his physical exam, he told the examining doctor that he had a medical ailment that would hinder his performance as a soldier. "Oh, what is that?" the doctor asked.

"I've got no guts," Joey cracked.

He lied.

Made in USA - Crawfordsville, IN
35411_9781587365836
01.26.2023 1845